THE
SIMCHA
COOKBOOK

13-Digit ISBN: 978-1-64643-141-0
10-Digit ISBN: 1-64643-141-3

This book may be ordered by mail from the publisher. Please include $5.99 for postage and handling.
Please support your local bookseller first!

Books published by Cider Mill Press Book Publishers are available at special discounts for bulk purchases in the United States by corporations, institutions, and other organizations. For more information, please contact the publisher.

Cider Mill Press Book Publishers
"Where good books are ready for press"
PO Box 454
12 Spring Street
Kennebunkport, Maine 04046

Visit us online!
cidermillpress.com

Typography: Sofia Pro, Arboria Black

All photographs by Adrien Shemtov, except front cover image and pages 174 and 177, which are used under official license from Shutterstock.com.

Front cover recipes: Pumpkin Baba Ghanoush: page 21; Crispy Salmon Rice: page 36; Bumble Bee Hummus: page 88; Thick Tahini: page 108; Couscous Arancini: page 120; kebab: not included; sambusak: not included.
Back cover recipes: Yemenite Fried Chicken: page 227; Yemenite Hot Sauce: page 111; Green Zhoug: page 101; Red Zhoug: page 99; Moroccan Carrots: page 76; Pinto Bean Fūl: page 152.

Printed in China
2 3 4 5 6 7 8 9 0

THE
SIMCHA
COOKBOOK

OVER 100 MODERN ISRAELI RECIPES, BLENDING MEDITERRANEAN AND MIDDLE EASTERN FLAVORS

AVI SHEMTOV

PHOTOGRAPHY BY ADRIEN SHEMTOV

CIDER MILL
PRESS

BOOK
PUBLISHERS
KENNEBUNKPORT, MAINE

CONTENTS

CUISINE AT A CROSSROADS

It was 1949, somewhere just outside of Istanbul, Turkey. My father's uncle, Yona, whom he would later be named for, had just been stabbed to death in the street. My grandfather, a quiet and physically unimposing man, charted a course for his family. His wife, my grandmother, had just given birth to their sixth child. They were accumulating wealth thanks to their thriving farm, but there was a growing sense that they would never be safe in their homeland. My grandfather decided that they would make the pilgrimage to the newly formed land of Israel. They left immediately.

Carrying only necessities and the money they would spend entirely securing their safe passage, they traveled to their new home. When they arrived, they found a one-bedroom apartment with a dirt floor, among the other poor Sephardic Jews who had come to seek refuge from an increasingly hostile Arab world. They were Arabs, culturally speaking, but now they would be Israelis.

In 1950, two years after the nation of Israel was created, my father was born. My grandfather had opened a stall in the Machane Yehuda Market, walking distance from their apartment. Food was scarce. Space was tight. The dream of a new life had not yet become a reality for my family.

My grandmother was an imposing woman by any measure. She was tall and strong. She was hard and tough. She was a true matriarch. Food was her warmth. My grandmother mastered the art of peasant food. She turned simple and humble ingredients into dishes with deep flavor that soothed your soul and transformed your circumstances. It was no accident that my grandmother was called Simcha, her cooking brought joy and celebration.

I never spent a lot of time with my grandmother. My father was the only member of his family to leave Israel for America, and I grew up far away from our family. She passed away when I was four. I remember where I was standing when my father got the news. My mom packed his suitcase while I watched him sob. It was the only time I'd seen him cry.

Still, my grandmother and I have always been close. My father has spent his life cooking. He started teaching me to cook when I was very young. Long before I understood technique or science, I understood that my dad's Americanized dishes possessed my grandmother's Turkish soul. The way toasted paprika melts into olive oil when eggplant salad is folded together is no different than the way chorizo sweats and coats farfalle. That is what I learned to love about cooking food, making it feel like something.

Israeli cuisine is at a crossroads. Great chefs have introduced the many cultural dishes of the nation to the world's stage and America has embraced our unique blend of Mediterranean and Middle Eastern foods. Some of the best restaurants in America pay tribute to Israel and all that it has to offer. Modern Israeli food is everywhere.

In true Israeli fashion, I have little interest in the status quo. I want to innovate. I want to create. I want to feature the fearless flavors of Israeli food and take them somewhere new. I want to reimagine; I want to cross boundaries. Now is the time to move Israeli cuisine past the modern and into the future.

With far less urgency and under much less dramatic circumstances, I find myself asking the same questions that my grandfather asked that night in Turkey: What's next? Where do I go from here? How do I move forward? Just as he did almost seventy years ago, I find my answer in Simcha.

MEZZE, SALADS, SIDES & STAPLES

At Simcha we don't serve traditional courses, instead we flood the table with small plates and spreads and breads. We graze, and we share. Mezze and salad courses overlap; sides are the norm and entrees are the rarity. Staples like sauces, spreads, and dips can be a snack, or the whole meal. Eating is a ritual, and so often it is a moment meant to bring people to the table for a shared experience.

ROASTED & STUFFED SARDINES, see page 16

ROASTED & STUFFED SARDINES

This is an ideal way to use up leftover bread, which absorbs so much flavor in this preparation. Keep in mind that the sardines' bones are edible.

5 WHOLE FRESH SARDINES

3 TABLESPOONS EXTRA VIRGIN OLIVE OIL, DIVIDED

½ WHITE ONION, CHOPPED

¼ CUP CHOPPED CELERY

1 TEASPOON KOSHER SALT

1 TABLESPOON PAPRIKA

1 PINCH CUMIN

2 GARLIC CLOVES, MINCED

2 TABLESPOONS WATER

¼ CUP CHOPPED PARSLEY

1 CUP CUBED DAY-OLD BREAD

TAHINI, TO SERVE

1. Clean the sardines by making an incision in their belly from head to tail. Remove the guts and, carefully, snap their spine at the neck and tail. This will leave the sardine intact enough to hold shape when roasted. Rinse and set aside.

2. Add 2 tablespoons olive oil to a medium-sized frying pan over medium-high heat. When the oil begins to shimmer add the onion, celery, salt, paprika, cumin, and garlic. Allow the onions to sweat for 4 to 5 minutes, or until they become translucent.

3. Add water and simmer for 3 or 4 minutes. Add the parsley and bread. Stir often, allowing the bread to absorb the liquids and brown a bit. After 5 minutes remove from heat.

4. Preheat oven to 450°F.

5. Place sardines in a cast-iron skillet, keeping them nestled into each other as much as possible so they help each other hold shape. Stuff the sardines' bellies with the stuffing. Sprinkle them with the remainder of the olive oil and roast for 15 to 20 minutes, or until they reach an internal temperature of 145°F.

6. Serve hot with tahini.

OLIVE OIL-POACHED FLUKE

At Simcha, we bring in the whole fluke when they're plentiful. Breaking them down is a task, but the meat is fresh and beautiful. We treat it very delicately, using sous vide and only really good olive oil, adding clean flavors at the very end. Similar to crudo, this dish highlights the beauty of stellar ingredients.

8 OZ. FLUKE FILLET

1¼ CUP EXTRA-VIRGIN OLIVE OIL, DIVIDED

1 TEASPOON KOSHER SALT

½ LEMON

1 PINCH BLACK PEPPER

1 PINCH PARSLEY, FOR GARNISH

1. Using an immersion circulator (I use a Joule) submerged in a container filled with water, set temperature to 145°F.

2. In a zip lock bag, place the fluke and 1 cup extra-virgin olive oil. Place into the water, making sure to remove all air from the bag and leave the top of the bag outside of the water—no water in the bag; I find the best method is to leave the bag open and slowly submerge it, allowing the water to create a vacuum seal, then chip clip the bag to the side of your container. Sous vide for 1 hour.

3. Leaving the top of the bag open, refrigerate the fish for at least 1 hour.

4. Slice the fish into 1-inch thick pieces and plate chilled. Season with salt and pepper, pool the remainder of the olive oil around the fish, garnish with parsley, and squeeze lemon over the top.

OLIVE OIL POACHED FLUKE, see page 17

CHICKEN LIVER MOUSSE

Some dishes are classics for a reason, like this velvety, rich spread. Even people put off by the idea of eating chicken liver will be surprised by how much they enjoy this.

1 TABLESPOON UNSALTED BUTTER

8 OZ. CHICKEN LIVER, CHOPPED

2 TABLESPOONS CHOPPED WHITE ONION

1 TEASPOON KOSHER SALT

1 TEASPOON BLACK PEPPER

2 TABLESPOONS BALSAMIC VINEGAR

3 OZ. HEAVY CREAM

1. Add butter to a large frying pan over medium-high heat. When the butter begins to foam add liver and onion, season with salt and pepper, and cook, stirring frequently, until the liver is no longer pink.

2. Place the mixture in a food processor. Puree and slowly add the balsamic vinegar. Next, slowly add the cream. Once the mixture is smooth, scoop it into a container with a lid and refrigerate it, uncovered, to set.

3. After an hour, put the lid on the container and leave it in the refrigerator for a few more hours to let the liver fully set.

4. Serve cold or at room temperature with crackers or grilled bread.

PUMPKIN BABA GHANOUSH

This was one of the first dishes I created when the Simcha concept began to take form. It resonates with our customers because of its deep New England roots and truly Israeli flavors. Pumpkin as a savory dish is profoundly Israeli, and Middle Eastern in general. It takes a little time and effort to cook and chop just right, but it's worth the work.

1 LARGE PUMPKIN

2 CUPS THICK TAHINI (SEE PAGE 108)

½ CUP CHOPPED PARSLEY

1. Heat the grill to high.

2. Once the grill is fully heated, set the pumpkin on it and allow to char for 30 minutes to an hour before turning the pumpkin onto its side, where it can stay for 20 to 30 minutes. Continue to rotate the pumpkin until all sides have charred and the pumpkin is completely soft all the way through.

3. Remove the pumpkin from the grill and, while still hot, split it open. Use a spoon to scoop out the soft flesh and remove the seeds and any parts that are not fully softened.

4. On a large cutting board, chop the cooked pumpkin flesh until fully minced, using an up and down chopping motion. Next, fold in the tahini and parsley, using a knife. Once the pumpkin, tahini, and parsley are fully incorporated, scrape the baba off the board and onto a bowl with a rim.

5. Serve room temperature with warm bread.

PEARL COUSCOUS MAC & CHEESE, see page 24

PEARL COUSCOUS MAC & CHEESE

Pearl couscous, often called Ben Gurion's rice in Israel (Gurion was a former prime minister), is a small, tender pasta. The texture and size make using it for mac and cheese super tasty.

1 CUP PEARL COUSCOUS

1 TABLESPOON UNSALTED BUTTER

1 TABLESPOON WHITE FLOUR

1 CUP WHOLE MILK

½ CUP SHREDDED PEPPER JACK CHEESE

1 TABLESPOON CHOPPED PARSLEY

1 PINCH KOSHER SALT

1 PINCH GRANULATED GARLIC

1 PINCH NUTMEG

1. In a medium-sized pot boil 5 cups of water. Once the water is boiling, add the pearl couscous and boil for 10 to 12 minutes, or until tender. Strain and set aside.

2. Add the butter to a small saucepan over medium heat. Once the butter has melted whisk in the flour and cook until a paste forms. Slowly pour in one-third of the milk and whisk until smooth and repeat with the rest of the milk. Add the cheese and seasoning and mix slowly.

3. Once the cheese has fully melted add the couscous and serve hot.

MUSHROOM & THYME CHOWDER

Mushroom soup is super New England fall. The thyme adds a twist to this classic and the aged provolone imparts a pleasant funkiness. All in all, this soup is perfect for rainy days and summer evenings alike.

2 TABLESPOONS UNSALTED BUTTER

2 SPRIGS THYME

8 OZ. FRESH MUSHROOMS, SLICED

1 TABLESPOON ALL-PURPOSE FLOUR

4 CUPS MILK

½ CUP GRATED AGED PROVOLONE CHEESE

1. Add the butter to a medium-sized saucepot over medium-high heat. Once the butter is melted turn to low heat and add the thyme. Allow to infuse for 5 minutes or so and remove the thyme.

2. Return the heat to medium-high, add the mushrooms to the melted butter, and sauté for 2 minutes or so. Next, add the flour and whisk until the contents of the pan become pasty.

3. Pour in the milk ¼ cup at a time, whisking to prevent clumping. Stir often to prevent the milk from burning, and after the soup begins to thicken add the grated cheese.

4. Stir until the chowder becomes thick. Serve hot.

MUSHROOM & THYME CHOWDER, see page 25

CHICKPEA POUTINE, see page 30

CHICKPEA POUTINE

My introduction to panisse, or chickpea fries, came from my good friends Mark and Amy who had them at a bistro in DC and thought they'd fit well on the menu at my food truck, The Chubby Chickpea. In that environment, they're served simply with a dipping sauce and the batter is a little bit tighter, producing a fluffier but less gooey fry. At Simcha we use them as the base for a fun play on the Canadian classic poutine, taking advantage of the short rib meat from our entrée portioning.

1 CUP CHICKPEA FLOUR

2 TEASPOONS KOSHER SALT

1 TEASPOON GRANULATED GARLIC

2 TABLESPOONS DRIED PARSLEY

1 PINCH CUMIN

2 CUPS BOILING WATER

8 OZ. BRAISED SHORT RIB (SEE PAGE 214)

½ CUP FETA CHEESE

CANOLA OIL, FOR FRYING

1. In a medium-size bowl combine the dry ingredients. Add the boiling water and whisk until the batter is smooth and is at stiff peaks. Pour into a small baking pan about an inch deep to set.

2. After about 1 hour turn the baking pan upside down over a cutting board. The chickpea mixture should come out in a whole piece. Using a sharp knife, cut the single piece into 1-inch thick rectangles.

3. In a large pot heat at least 4 inches of canola oil to 350°F. Once the oil is hot enough, fry the chickpea fries for approximately 4 minutes, until browned and crispy on the outside. Turn after 2 minutes if necessary.

4. Break up the braised short rib and add it and ½ cup water to a small saucepan over high heat. Simmer the beef until the water reduces by half and then set aside.

5. On a plate with a rim or in a shallow bowl, place half of the chickpea fries in a Jenga-style frame. Using tongs or a slotted spoon, place half the short rib meat over the fries and then add half of the gravy. Sprinkle half of the feta over the fries. Repeat for a second portion. Serve hot.

ENSALADA DE PULPO

Octopus was the very first dish we created for the Simcha menu and, when it is on the menu, we believe it is where we stand out the very most. Super tender tentacles are the trick, and we get there by simply breaking down the protein. This version uses our herb-filled verde sauce paired with astringent quick pickles for texture contrast. Once you've cooked the octopus you can pair it with whatever salad you'd love to create!

1 WHOLE OCTOPUS, FROZEN

3 RADISHES

2 TEASPOONS KOSHER SALT

1 CUP WHITE VINEGAR, DIVIDED

1 PEAR

½ CUP VERDE SAUCE

2 CUPS MESCLUN GREENS

VERDE SAUCE:

4 MEDIUM JALAPEÑOS, CHOPPED

1 WHITE ONION, CHOPPED

1 TABLESPOON CUMIN

1 TEASPOON WHITE PEPPER

1 TABLESPOON KOSHER SALT

1 TABLESPOON CHOPPED CILANTRO

1 TABLESPOON CHOPPED PARSLEY

2 CUPS WHITES VINEGAR

1 CUP WATER

1. Fill a pot, large enough to fully submerge the octopus under water, with water and bring it to a hard boil. Once the water is boiling, add the frozen octopus and cover the pot. Boil for 1 hour and 40 minutes (if the water reduces too much add water as needed). By the time you remove the octopus from the water, it should be tender enough to fall apart when grabbed by tongs. Separate the tentacles and put them aside to cool.

2. While the octopus is boiling, cut ⅛-inch thick radish slices, salt them, and cover them with half the vinegar in a bowl. In a separate bowl place ¼-inch thick pear slices, skin on, and also salt and submerge those in the remainder of the vinegar.

3. When you are ready to plate, heat a frying pan or grill and sear each octopus tentacle; if using a pan, add a few drops of extra-virgin olive oil so the octopus doesn't stick to the pan.

4. To serve, spoon 1 tablespoon of Verde Sauce onto the plate and place a full tentacle alongside it. Put the greens in a small pile on the plate and add radish and pear slices.

VERDE SAUCE

1. Add all of the ingredients to a medium saucepan over high heat, bring to a boil, then reduce to medium-high heat amd simmer for 40 minutes.

2. Allow to cool for 15 to 20 minutes, then process in a blender or food processor. Use a course strainer to remove any large pulp or food particles. Keeps in refrigerator for up to 2 weeks.

ENSALADA DE PULPO, see page 31

CRISPY SALMON RICE, see page 36

CRISPY SALMON RICE

When cutting sides of salmon into portions, or making lox, I always remove the belly. This makes for more evenly cooked salmon, but it also lets me keep the most precious part of the fish to incorporate in other dishes in smaller amounts. I feel strongly about this philosophy as it ties into my grandmother's kitchen and the way that my father has always cooked: rich ingredients go a long way in hearty peasant dishes. This rice is a beautiful side or a weekday main.

2 TABLESPOONS CANOLA OIL

½ WHITE ONION, MINCED

¼ CUP SLICED SCALLIONS

¼ CUP CHOPPED PARSLEY

2 TEASPOONS KOSHER SALT

2 CUPS COOKED WHITE RICE, COLD

6 OZ. SALMON BELLY

1 TABLESPOON POMEGRANATE MOLASSES

1 TABLESPOON APPLE CIDER VINEGAR

1. Add the oil to a large frying pan over high heat; use the largest pan available as the surface area is critical for this recipe. When the oil begins to shimmer add the onion, scallions, parsley, and salt. Stirring often, cook until the onions are translucent.

2. Add the rice and stir frequently, until the rice gets crispy, about 3 to 5 minutes. Add the salmon, turn down the heat to medium-high and allow to warm through, about 3 minutes.

3. In a small bowl, whisk the molasses and vinegar together. Before removing the rice from heat add this mixture to the rice and stir. Remove from heat and serve hot.

YIELD: 4 SERVINGS   **TOTAL TIME:** 1 HOUR AND 30 MINUTES

TURKISH EGGPLANT SALAD

At its core, our food is Turkish in one form or another. My grandmother was Turkish through and through, and my father's food bears the same fingerprints. Our eggplant salad is more than likely the purest show of our Turkish heritage: unmistakably garlic heavy, smoky, earthy. It is also arguably my favorite dish to cook, behind shakshuka (see page 149).

2 LARGE EGGPLANTS

2 TABLESPOONS OLIVE OIL

3 MEDIUM TOMATOES, LARGE DICE

1 WHITE ONION, JULIENNED

4 GARLIC CLOVES

1 TABLESPOON PAPRIKA

1 TEASPOON KOSHER SALT

1 TEASPOON CUMIN

1 TEASPOON CAYENNE

½ CUP CHOPPED PARSLEY

1. In either a 450°F oven or on a grill set to high, char eggplants until they are fully softened and somewhat shriveled; this not an exact science, but longer is better, 40 minutes to 1 hour. Allow to cool.

2. Add the oil to a large frying pan over high heat. When the oil begins to shimmer add the tomatoes and onions, followed by the remainder of the ingredients, except the parsley. Cook for approximately 20 minutes, stirring occasionally. Remove from heat.

3. Split open the eggplants and scoop out the soft flesh and fold it i into the tomato mixture, adding the parsley as you go. Serve at room temperature.

TURKISH EGGPLANT SALAD, see page 37

EGGPLANT RINGS

Fried eggplant is a classic comfort food in our culture, something mothers or grandmothers make as they cook, which kids running around stop to scoop up hot and gobble down. We use a pastry cutter to remove the skin from this crispy and gooey treat, and create a very cool and unique shape in the process!

1 LARGE EGGPLANT

2 EGGS, BEATEN

1 CUP ALL-PURPOSE FLOUR

1 CUP PANKO

1 TABLESPOON SALT

1 TABLESPOON CRACKED BLACK PEPPER

2 CUPS CANOLA OIL

2 OZ. RED ZHOUG (SEE PAGE 99)

2 OZ. KETCHUP

1. Slice off the top and bottom of the eggplant and discard. Next, slice the entire eggplant into ½ inch-thick horizontal slices. Using circular dough cutters, cut the eggplant first into circles then remove the center, creating rings that have about an inch of eggplant inside them.

2. Set up 3 bowls, one with flour, one with egg wash, one with panko (seasoned with salt and pepper). Dip a ring into the flour, then the egg, and lastly the panko, coating the ring entirely. Set the coated ring on a sheet pan and repeat until all of the rings are coated.

3. Add the canola oil to a cast-iron skillet (ideally less than 4 inches deep) over high heat. Once the oil reaches 375°F fry 4 or 5 rings at a time. Allow the rings to cook for about 2 minutes, or until browned, and then flip the rings and cook for an additional 2 minutes, or until browned. Remove, place on a cooling rack, and repeat until all of the rings are fried.

4. In a small bowl, combine the zhoug and ketchup and mix well. Serve the rings hot with this spicy sauce on the side.

SHAVED SNAP PEA SALAD

This salad depends on the thin slicing of the snap peas and the quality of the honey to fully blossom into the beautiful salad it is meant to be. At its best, this is a vibrant mix of sweet and acidic, herby and crunchy.

1 LB. SNAP PEAS

1 TABLESPOON CHOPPED DILL

1 TABLESPOON CHOPPED BASIL

1 TABLESPOON CHOPPED MINT

2 TEASPOONS HONEY

¼ CUP WHITE VINEGAR

1 TEASPOON KOSHER SALT

1 TABLESPOON CRUSHED TOASTED WALNUTS

1. Using a sharp knife, stack 4 snap peas at a time and cut thin slices on the bias. Once all of the snap peas are cut, put them into a medium-sized bowl.

2. By hand, mix all of the other ingredients into the peas, making sure to thoroughly incorporate them all.

3. Allow the salad to stand for at least 30 minutes, and up to an hour, before serving.

SHAVED SNAP PEA SALAD, see page 47

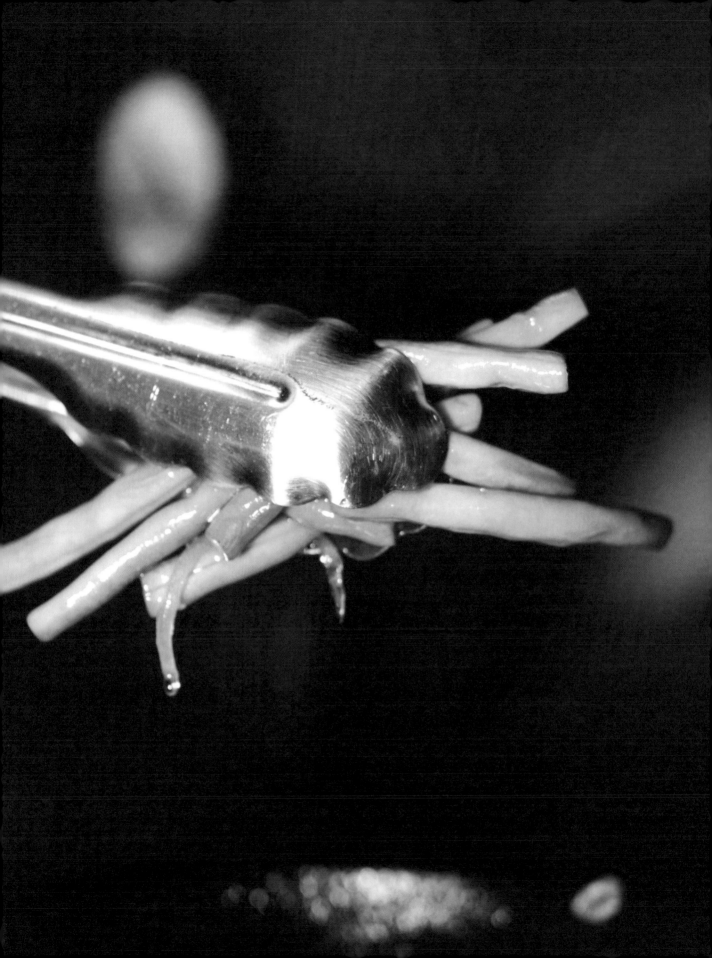

PICKLED GREEN BEANS

I love to pickle vegetables. Truth be told, I love acid and vinegar in general. Like so many things in our kitchen, we started pickling green beans to keep product from going to waste and make a delicious staff snack. They evolved and ended up on salads and into wood-oven dishes. Here we simply roast and serve them for a crunchy, different take on a classic.

1 LB. GREEN BEANS, SNIPPED

2 TABLESPOONS CHOPPED DILL

2 GARLIC CLOVES, MINCED

1 TABLESPOON KOSHER SALT

1 TABLESPOON SUGAR

2 CUPS WHITE VINEGAR

1 TABLESPOON EXTRA-VIRGIN OLIVE OIL

1 TABLESPOON HONEY

1. In a large container with a lid, combine the green beans, dill, garlic, salt, and sugar. Pour the vinegar over the green beans, mix well, and refrigerate for 24 to 48 hours.

2. After at least 24 hours have passed, preheat the oven to 450°F. Remove the green beans from the liquid (I save the liquid to quick pickle onions) and place them on a sheet pan. Toss in olive oil and roast for 20 minutes, or until browned.

3. Remove from the oven, drizzle with honey, and serve hot.

GRILLED CANTALOUPE, see page 48

GRILLED CANTALOUPE

A grill master friend of mine taught me a few years back that a grill should be used to flavor and impact a dish, rather than simply as a tool to cook food. By grilling cantaloupe, we completely change its texture and add a charred bitterness to its inherent sweetness. Married with creamy mozzarella and tangy balsamic, this is a very simple yet wonderfully compex dish.

1 CANTALOUPE

1 TABLESPOON EXTRA-VIRGIN OLIVE OIL

4 OZ. FRESH MOZZARELLA CHEESE, TORN

1 TABLESPOON BALSAMIC VINEGAR REDUCTION

1 TABLESPOON CHOPPED PARSLEY

1. Heat the grill to high.

2. Remove the rind from the cantaloupe, halve, remove the seeds, and then cut the cantaloupe into ½-inch-thick slices.

3. Toss the cantaloupe slices in the oil and, once the grill is fully hot, grill the slices on both sides, approximately 1 ½ minutes per side, until grill marks are prominent and the cantaloupe is warmed through.

4. To serve, pile the warm slices onto a plate, scatter mozzarella over the fruit, drizzle the balsamic reduction over everything, and garnish with parsley.

FRIED FETA

For the Simcha team, an R & D trip to Nashville was not only an incredibly fun time full of lasting memories, but it also yielded food experiences that changed our perspectives. Of all places, it was Nashville where we first ate pan-fried feta and the texture was astounding. We chose to batter it for the crunch, and we turned it into a salad of sorts by sitting it atop warm greens.

1 CUP ALL-PURPOSE FLOUR

1 TEASPOON KOSHER SALT

1 TEASPOON BAKING POWDER

1 CUP WATER

2 CUPS CANOLA OIL, FOR FRYING

1 (½-INCH-THICK) BLOCK OF FETA CHEESE

1 TEASPOON EXTRA-VIRGIN OLIVE OIL

1 CUP GRAPE TOMATOES

½ HEAD OF ROMAINE LETTUCE

1 TABLESPOON BALSAMIC REDUCTION

1. Combine flour, salt, baking powder, and water in a small bowl and whisk thoroughly, making sure there are no lumps.

2. Add canola oil to a small saucepan over medium-high heat. Once the oil is hot enough to fry, carefully coat the block of feta in the batter.

3. Place the feta into the oil by first submerging half into the oil for 5 seconds, then releasing it so that it free floats. Fry for 1½ minutes on each side. Keep an eye on the feta; if the batter doesn't seal the feta will ooze out and this won't work. Once the feta has browned, set it on a cooling rack.

4. Separately, add the olive oil to a frying pan over high heat. Put the cherry tomatoes into the oil and allow them to blister for 2 to 3 minutes. Add the lettuce leaves and brown for about 1 minute.

5. To serve, place the lettuce in a shallow bowl, scatter the cherry tomatoes, and nest the fried block of feta on top. Drizzle with balsamic reduction.

FRIED FETA, see page 49

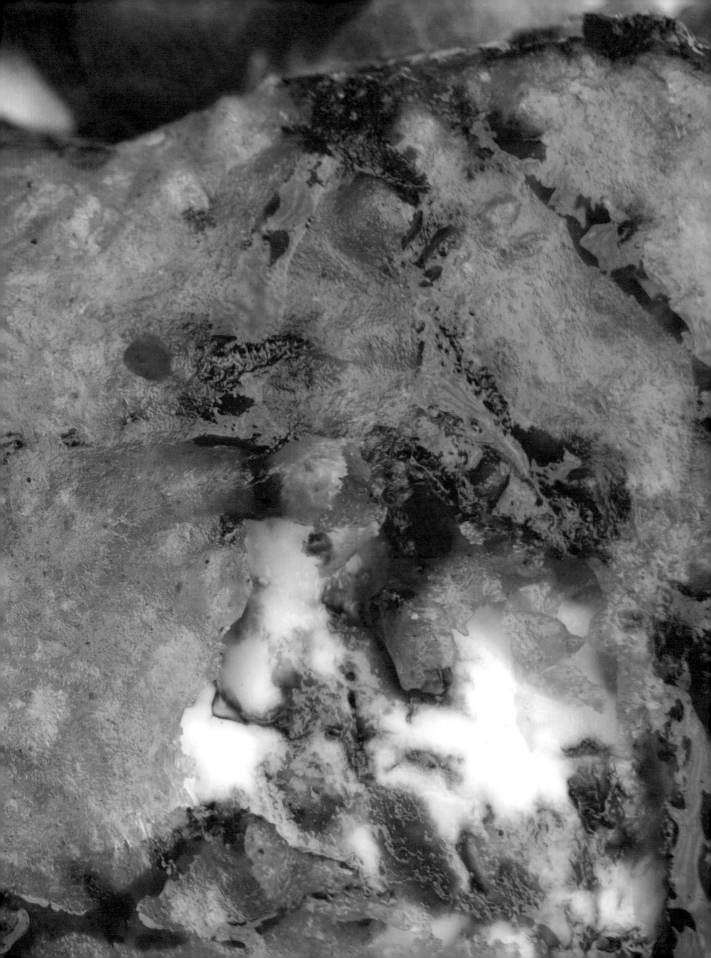

BLACK PEPPER-GLAZED ASPARAGUS, see page 54

BLACK PEPPER–GLAZED ASPARAGUS

Roasted sweet and savory asparagus makes a beautiful and nimble side. This version combines flavors from my grandmother's kitchen with the asparagus my wife's family makes at Easter.

10 STALKS ASPARAGUS, PLUS 1 TABLESPOON SHAVED ASPARAGUS

JUICE OF 1 LEMON

1 TABLESPOON WHITE SUGAR

1 TABLESPOON EXTRA-VIRGIN OLIVE OIL

1 TEASPOON KOSHER SALT

2 GARLIC CLOVES, MINCED

1 TEASPOON CRACKED BLACK PEPPER

SHAVED PARMESAN CHEESE, TO TASTE

1. Heat the broiler to high.

2. Cut off the woody asparagus ends (there should be a natural spot at which a stalk will break when bent firmly).

3. Combine lemon juice, sugar, olive oil, salt, and garlic in a bowl, mix well, and then coat the asparagus in this mixture.

4. Spread out the asparagus in an even layer on a sheet pan, sprinkle the pepper over the stalks, and broil until the stalks are beautifully browned, approximately 10 minutes.

5. To serve, place the asparagus on a plate in a single layer and cover with shaved Parmesan.

ROASTED RADICCHIO

Bitterness is an important flavor for the Jewish people and an important part of Israeli cuisine. Radicchio is certainly bitter, and in this salad, its bitterness is contrasted with the sweetness of balsamic vinegar, the salty sourness of capers, and the salty sweetness of feta. By roasting the radicchio, we add a complex caramelized aspect as well. It is a very simple salad with a very complicated flavor profile, which I think nails what Simcha is all about!

1 HEAD OF RADICCHIO

¼ CUP EXTRA-VIRGIN OLIVE OIL

1 TEASPOON KOSHER SALT

¼ CUP BALSAMIC VINEGAR

1 TABLESPOON CAPERS

¼ CUP FETA CHEESE

1. Preheat the oven to 450°F.

2. Cut the radicchio head in half and remove the stem. Peel the leaves apart and, in a medium-size bowl, toss them in the olive oil. Arrange the leaves on a sheet pan and sprinkle with salt. Roast for 10 to 15 minutes, until the leaves brown and are slightly wilted. Remove from the oven, leaving the oven on.

3. Evenly distribute the vinegar and capers over the radicchio and return the sheet pan to the oven for 5 to 10 minutes, until the vinegar starts to bubble.

4. To serve, place the leaves and capers, while hot, onto a plate or into a salad bowl, and sprinkle with the feta.

SEARED EGGPLANT, see page 58

SEARED EGGPLANT

Cooking is a collaborative process and many of the cooks who have worked at Simcha have added their personal touch to our style and our menu. Our seared eggplant, a continually popular dish, was the brainchild of our opening sous chef, Frank Drury. Frank used Japanese and Thai eggplants in his original dish, but we've adapted it to be a little more accessible to New England-grown ingredients.

1 CUP WOOD CHIPS

1 ONION, QUARTERED

2 TEASPOONS KOSHER SALT, DIVIDED

¼ CUP VEGETABLE OIL

1 SMALL EGGPLANT

1 RED BELL PEPPER

¼ CUP BALSAMIC VINEGAR

1. Place the wood chips in a small cast-iron pan, light them on fire, place the cast-iron pan into an oven-safe pan, and place the onion pieces beside the cast iron. Cover the pan with foil. After 20 minutes or so remove the onion from the pan and puree in a food processor. Add 1 teaspoon kosher salt, stir, and set aside.

2. Cut both the eggplant and the red pepper into ½-inch squares. Add the oil to a frying pan over high heat. When the oil begins to shimmer add the eggplant. Let the eggplant brown on one side, approximately 1 minute, and then turn the pieces over, adding the red pepper. After another minute add the balsamic vinegar to the pan and toss the vegetables.

3. To serve, spoon even portions of the onion puree onto 4 plates and top with the vegetables.

ROASTED OKRA

Growing up we ate okra all the time, but almost exclusively in stews (okra thickens soups and stews) and kubbe. Roasted okra contrasts a crispy exterior with a gooey inside.

2 TABLESPOONS EXTRA-VIRGIN OLIVE OIL

6 OKRA PODS

1 TEASPOON KOSHER SALT

1 TEASPOON CRACKED BLACK PEPPER

1 TEASPOON BROWN SUGAR

1 TEASPOON WHITE VINEGAR

¼ CUP GOAT CHEESE, TO SERVE

1. Add the oil to a cast-iron pan over high heat. When the oil begins to shimmer add the okra, salt, and pepper. Brown the okra on all sides and remove it from the pan, leaving the pan on the stove but turning off the heat.

2. Put the sugar and vinegar in the pan and stir. The hot pan will quickly cause the mixture to turn syrupy.

3. To serve, spread the goat cheese on a small plate, arrange the okra in a line, and drizzle the vinegar syrup on top.

ROASTED OKRA, see page 59

PECAN MUHAMMARA

Typically, muhammara is made using walnuts, but we substitute pecans as an ode to my grandmother (on my mother's side) who loved pecan pie. This version is mildly spicy and has a texture more like baba ghanoush than hummus.

2 RED BELL PEPPERS

¼ CUP PECANS

1 TEASPOON KOSHER SALT

1 TEASPOON ALEPPO PEPPER

½ CUP EXTRA-VIRGIN OLIVE OIL

JUICE OF 1 LEMON

1 TABLESPOON POMEGRANATE MOLASSES

¼ CUP BREAD CRUMBS

1 TABLESPOON CHOPPED PARSLEY, TO GARNISH

1. On a grill or in a hot pan, char the red peppers on all sides. Remove them from the heat, place them into a bowl, and cover the bowl with plastic wrap. After 15 minutes, remove the plastic and peel the skin off the peppers. Remove the seeds, stems, and pith (the white parts that separate each section of the pepper).

2. Combine the peppers and pecans in a food processor and blend. Add the salt, Aleppo pepper, olive oil, lemon juice, and molasses and blend. With the food processor off, fold in the bread crumbs.

3. Serve cold or at room temperature.

GRAPEFRUIT & FENNEL SALAD, see page 66

GRAPEFRUIT & FENNEL SALAD

Citrus and fennel make for amazing culinary partners. Grapefruit's tang really pulls together all of the fresh herbs, anise flavor, and honey in this salad.

½ **WHITE ONION**

2 **FENNEL STALKS, WITH FRONDS**

1 **MEDIUM APPLE**

1 **TEASPOON CHOPPED DILL**

1 **TEASPOON CHOPPED MINT**

1 **TABLESPOON CHOPPED PARSLEY**

1 **TABLESPOON HONEY**

3 **TABLESPOONS WHITE VINEGAR**

1 **JALAPEÑO, THINLY SLICED**

1 **GRAPEFRUIT, SUPREMED**

1. Using a mandolin or a sharp knife shave the white onion, fennel, and apple into very thin slices (⅛ inch). Chop the fennel fronds.

2. In a medium bowl combine the sliced items and chopped fronds with the herbs, honey and vinegar.

3. Add the jalapeño and grapefruit and lightly toss. Serve immediately.

ROASTED TOMATO PESTO CAPRESE

At Simcha our wood-fire oven is the centerpiece of the restaurant and, in addition to our warm pita, is where a lot of our unique takes on vegetable preparations come from. At home, it's not possible to get to 900°F, but the same principles apply to these dishes: use a hot oven to change the textures, getting a very different bite.

½ **CUP BASIL**

½ **CUP FRESH SPINACH**

2 GARLIC CLOVES

½ **CUP EXTRA-VIRGIN OLIVE OIL**

½ **CUP PARMESAN CHEESE**

½ **CUP BALSAMIC VINEGAR**

2 MEDIUM-SIZED TOMATOES

6 OZ. FRESH MOZZARELLA CHEESE

1. Preheat the oven to 450°F.

2. Combine the basil, spinach, garlic, oil (reserving 1 tablespoon), and Parmesan in a food processor or blender and blend until smooth. Set aside.

3. Add the vinegar to a small saucepan over medium-high heat. As soon as it bubbles turn down the heat to medium and reduce the vinegar by half, approximately 6 to 8 minutes. Let cool completely before using.

4. Slice the tomatoes about 1/8-inch-thick, coat them in reserved oil, and spread across a sheet pan, making sure not to stack the tomatoes. Place mozzarella in chunks or slices around the tomatoes and bake for 10 minutes, or until the cheese is golden and the tomatoes have browned.

5. To serve, use a spatula to place the tomatoes and cheese on a plate. Spoon the pesto in globs onto the tomatoes and drizzle the balsamic reduction over the top.

SUMAC & APPLE-ROASTED CAULIFLOWER, see page 70

SUMAC & APPLE-ROASTED CAULIFLOWER

Whole roasted cauliflower is a staple of the modern Israeli kitchen. By roasting the cauliflower covered it gets very soft while also absorbing the onion, apple, and sumac flavors. This soft but crispy version is sweet and creamy.

1 APPLE, PEELED AND QUARTERED

1 ONION, QUARTERED

1 TABLESPOON SUMAC

1 TABLESPOON KOSHER SALT

1 TABLESPOON SUGAR

½ CUP WATER

1 WHOLE CAULIFLOWER

2 TABLESPOONS HONEY

2 TABLESPOONS TAHINI

1. Preheat the oven to 400°F.

2. Combine the apple, onion, sumac, salt, sugar, and water in a food processor and pulse.

3. Using a sharp knife, remove any leaves from the cauliflower and square off the stem. Place the cauliflower head in a roasting pan and coat with the apple and onion mixture. Wrap with foil and roast for 45 minutes, until the cauliflower is soft enough to cut into with a fork. Set the oven to 450°F and finish the cauliflower for 10 more minutes uncovered.

4. To serve, set the cauliflower on a rimmed plate and drizzle with honey and tahini.

MARINATED EGGPLANT SALAD

Marinating eggplant after it has been grilled is a trick I use to pack in flavor while also imparting great texture. This super acidic, herbaceous salad is a complete change of pace from our more traditional Turkish eggplant salad.

1 EGGPLANT, SLICED INTO ½-INCH-THICK ROUNDS

½ CUP OLIVE OIL

4 GARLIC CLOVES, MINCED

1 TABLESPOON CHOPPED DILL

1 TABLESPOON CHOPPED BASIL

1 TABLESPOON KOSHER SALT

½ CUP WHITE VINEGAR

1 CUP HALVED CHERRY TOMATOES

2 SHALLOTS, JULIENNED

1. Heat up the grill, or a frying pan. Using a pastry brush, oil the eggplant slices and sear them for 3 minutes on each side, or until the eggplant is mildly charred. After the second side is charred, place the eggplant slices in a medium-sized bowl.

2. Add the garlic, herbs, salt, vinegar, and any remaining extra-virgin olive oil, to the eggplant. Add the tomatoes and shallots and mix well.

3. Refrigerate for at least 2 hours, and up to 5 days. Serve cold.

MARINATED EGGPLANT SALAD, see page 71

MOROCCAN CARROTS

Growing up, the carrots we ate were cut into medallions and stewed in a heavily spiced broth. The flavors of cinnamon and cayenne were dreamy, but hindsight being 20/20 they were often overpowered by the mushy texture of the carrots. Alongside stewed or braised meat they worked, but as a standalone dish they were forgettable. Eating at Alon Shaya's first Israeli restaurant with Jewish food historian Jeff Gabel my eyes were opened. Combining the French searing technique with the Norht African flavor profiles these carrots were awoken. At Simcha, we use local honey and sesame seeds to complete the evolution.

2 LARGE CARROTS, PEELED

1 TABLESPOON CANOLA OIL

1 TABLESPOON MOROCCAN SPICE (SEE PAGE 116)

2 TEASPOONS TAHINI

2 TEASPOONS HONEY

2 PINCHES WHITE SESAME SEEDS, TO GARNISH (OPTIONAL)

1. Cut the carrots into ½-inch-wide sticks, approximately 3 inches long.

2. Add the oil to a large frying pan over high heat. Once the oil begins to shimmer add the carrots to the pan, spreading them out as much as possible, and sprinkle with the Moroccan Spice. Sear both sides of the carrots until mildly blackened, approximately 3 minutes per side. Remove the carrots from the pan and place them on a paper towel-lined plate.

3. To serve, stack the carrots evenly on two small plates and drizzle a teaspoon of honey over the top of each stack, followed by a drizzle of tahini (drizzling the honey first ensures that it will melt on the hot carrots and not bead on the cool tahini). Garnish with sesame seeds, if desired.

DUKKAH BEETS, see page 78

YIELD: 2 SERVINGS   TOTAL TIME: 1 HOUR AND 30 MINUTES

DUKKAH BEETS

Dukkah is an Egyptian seed and nut blend often eaten in the same way that Americans might eat trail mix. At Simcha, we use our unique blend of seeds and nuts to contrast the texture of our seared beets. The result is a colorful and textural dish, unlike any beet preparation many people have had.

1 LARGE BEET

1 TABLESPOON CHOPPED WALNUTS

1 TABLESPOON CHOPPED HAZELNUTS

1 TEASPOON CRACKED BLACK PEPPER

1 TEASPOON POPPY SEEDS

1 TEASPOON BLACK SESAME SEEDS

1 PINCH KOSHER SALT

1 TABLESPOON CANOLA OIL

2 TABLESPOONS LABNEH

1 CINNAMON STICK

1 WHOLE FRESH CLOVE

1. Place the beet, skin on, in a medium pot over high heat with at least 5 cups of water. Boil the beet until a fork can easily pass through it, approximately 30 to 40 minutes.

2. Under running cold water peel off the skin and stems by hand; easiest to do this while the beet is still hot. Cut the beet into ¾-inch square chunks.

3. Add the nuts to a freezer bag and use a meat tenderizer or rolling pin to crush the nuts. Add the black pepper, seeds, and salt.

4. Add the oil to a frying pan over high heat. When the oil begins to shimmer sear the beets until they're deep brown on each side. Remove the beets from the oil and place them on a paper towel-lined plate.

5. To serve, spoon the labneh across the bottom of a small plate, pile the beets onto the labneh and sprinkle the Dukkah mix over the top. Grate a pinch of cinnamon and a pinch of clove across the pile.

GRILLED ROMAINE & SWEET POTATO

Some great advice a grill master once gave me was to use grilled ingredients within other dishes and to season or treat grilled items after they've been grilled, not just before. This romaine salad showcases the flavor of the grill, without being simply a grilled vegetable.

2 CUPS CANOLA OIL, FOR FRYING

1 CUP SHAVED SWEET POTATO SKINS

3 TEASPOONS KOSHER SALT, DIVIDED

2 TEASPOONS CRACKED BLACK PEPPER, DIVIDED

½ GREEN APPLE

½ CUP WHITE VINEGAR

1 ROMAINE HEART

2 TEASPOONS EXTRA-VIRGIN OLIVE OIL

1 TABLESPOON BALSAMIC VINEGAR

2 TABLESPOONS FETA CHEESE

1. Heat the oil in a small saucepan to approximately 350°F. Once the oil is hot, fry the sweet potato skins for approximately 1 minute, until golden brown and relatively crispy. Remove them from the oil and place them on a cooling rack. Season with 1 teaspoon salt and 1 teaspoon black pepper.

2. Cut the apples into ½-inch slices with the skin on. Place the apples in a small bowl and toss them with white vinegar and 1 teaspoon salt. Set aside. (These can be done ahead of time or while making the salad. For best results the apples should be refrigerated overnight, or for a few days.)

3. Heat up a grill or grill pan to high. Cut the stem off the romaine heart, pull apart the leaves, and coat the leaves with olive oil, 1 teaspoon salt, and 1 teaspoon black pepper. Grill the leaves until partially charred on each side, approximately 1 to 1½ minutes total. Don't let the leaves wilt.

4. To serve, spread out the romaine leaves on a rimmed plate, crumble the sweet potato skins over the lettuce, scatter the apple slices, and then splash the balsamic over the salad. Crumble the feta over the top.

GRILLED ROMAINE & SWEET POTATO, see page 79

AVICADO, see page 84

AVICADO

Chef Becca Arnold brought me my first warm avocado at Boston Calling a few years back—and it was an eye-opening bite. After a pop-up at Simcha Chef Dave Becker left behind roasted squash, so I mixed it with feta and shoved it in an avocado. The rest is history.

1 CUP SMALL CHUNKS BUTTERNUT SQUASH

2 TABLESPOONS EXTRA-VIRGIN OLIVE OIL, DIVIDED

1 TEASPOON KOSHER SALT.

1 TEASPOON FRESH BLACK PEPPER

2 RIPE AVOCADOS

½ CUP FETA CHEESE

2 TABLESPOONS SMOKED EGG AIOLI (SEE PAGE 102)

1. Preheat the oven to 450°F.

2. In a bowl, combine the squash with 1 tablespoon olive oil, salt, and pepper. Transfer the squash to a sheet pan and roast until lightly browned and soft enough to mush. Set aside.

3. Halve both avocados and remove their seeds. Using a spoon, remove approximately half of the avocado from the skin. Combine the removed avocado, the feta, and the roasted squash.

4. Divide the filling among the 4 avocado halves. Lightly brush the tops of the stuffed avocados with oil and place face up on a sheet pan.

5. Roast in the oven until the tops are browned.

6. To serve, drizzle with Smoked Egg Aioli.

FIG & GOAT CHEESE SALAD

People laugh, but I like to equate figs to grapes: the flavor in the fresh fruit is so different than the artificial stuff that it makes you wonder where they got the inspiration. Fresh figs and goat cheese is a classic combination, and wood-fired fruit with cheese is super Mediterranean. This salad has a twist with grilled orange slices and red wine reduction for a result that is familiar yet exciting.

1 CUP PINOT NOIR

1/4 CUP WHITE SUGAR

4 ORANGE SLICES

6 FRESH FIGS, HALVED

2 TABLESPOONS CREAMY GOAT CHEESE

1. Heat a grill or grill pan to high. Preheat the oven to 450°F.

2. Add the wine and sugar to a saucepan over medium-high heat, whisk until all the sugar dissolves, and simmer until the mixture reduces to syrupy consistency.

3. Sear the orange slices (unseasoned) until they're caramelized. Turn them over and repeat. Set aside.

4. Arrange the figs on a sheet pan face up and roast in the oven until they are lightly browned and soft.

5. To serve, set the orange slices on the bottom of a plate, place the roasted figs face-up around and on top of the oranges, sprinkle the goat cheese, and then drizzle the reduction.

FIG & GOAT CHEESE SALAD, **see page 85**

BUMBLE BEE HUMMUS

Hummus may have been the first solid food my parents ever fed me. Growing up it was for sure my dad's calling card. Once I became a chef in my own right, hummus quickly became a signature of mine as well. Ironically, as my career advanced and my hummus became more and more popular in the greater Boston area, mainstream hummus brands also improved and hummus became a household staple for Middle Easterners and Middle Americans alike.

When I opened Simcha this meant I had to reimagine the most iconic staple of my decade-long run with my food truck, The Chubby Chickpea. I began to search for New England-grown beans (chickpeas struggle to grow in our climate) and stumbled on the Bumble Bee Bean. They were everything I'd hoped for: unmistakably cool looking, hyper-local heritage beans, forgivingly neutral in flavor, and exceedingly creamy when cooked for 45 minutes. After playing around for a few weeks with my newly found toys, we stumbled on a super potent hummus. Reinventing what I'd felt I'd already perfected, for me, embodied what Simcha would become.

1 LB. BUMBLE BEE BEANS (OR WHITE BEANS)

¼ CUP EXTRA-VIRGIN OLIVE OIL, PLUS MORE TO SERVE

4 GARLIC CLOVES

2 TEASPOONS KOSHER SALT

JUICE OF 1½ LEMONS

1½ CUPS SOOM TAHINI

SESAME SEEDS (OPTIONAL)

PAPRIKA (OPTIONAL)

PINE NUTS (OPTIONAL)

PARSLEY (OPTIONAL)

1. Add the beans to a medium saucepan, cover them with at least 3 inches of water, and boil them for 45 minutes. I was taught by Chef Ohad Angel to throw a bean against the wall and see if it sticks. When it does, it's creamy enough for hummus. Pressing the beans between your fingers works too! Once your beans are completely soft, strain them quickly, but don't let them drip dry. The beans' water content will help to loosen up the tahini.

2. Place the beans in a food processor and puree for 15 seconds. Next add the olive oil, garlic, salt, and lemon juice. Process on high for 2 minutes, or until the beans become smooth. Lastly, add the tahini and process for another minute or so. The hummus should be creamy and smooth, but thick enough to hold a peak when spread onto a plate.

3. To serve, spoon the hummus onto a plate and create a divot, using the spoon. Traditionally hummus is spread in a circle so that a rim encases a thin layer within it. Either way, fill the center of the hummus with extra-virgin olive oil, parsley, pine nuts, paprika, and/or sesame seeds.

BABA GHANOUSH, see page 92

BABA GHANOUSH

Baba ghanoush is one of the many dishes my father was famous for when I was growing up and still, I refused to eat it. As an adult, and moreover as a chef, baba ghanoush has come to represent to me the beauty and skill of Middle Eastern food. As you can tell by the ingredient list, it's a very simple dish to make. Still, it can be very difficult if you don't understand a few very specific techniques. When made correctly, this baba ghanoush is creamy and smoky.

3 LARGE EGGPLANTS

¼ CUP CHOPPED PARSLEY

1 CUP THICK TAHINI SAUCE (SEE PAGE 108)

1 TEASPOON KOSHER SALT

1. On a charcoal grill, over a burner on your stove (yes, right on the burner), or in a fire pit char the eggplants, skin on. The eggplant will burn on the outside, but its skin will protect it and the inside will steam and smoke itself. Turn the eggplant every 10 minutes, until the inside feels completely mushy. Remove from the heat and let cool.

2. Using a sharp knife, slice the top off each eggplant and slice a seam from the top to the bottom. Use a spoon to remove all of the fully cooked insides, making sure not to remove any skin with it.

3. On a cutting board, chop the eggplant in an "up and down" motion, folding the parsley into the eggplant at the same time. Once the eggplant seems fully chopped, use the knife to fold in the tahini. Serve at room temperature.

FRIED BRUSSELS SPROUTS WITH TAHINI & FETA

Brussels sprouts are one of the many foods that I only acquired a taste for at the urging of my wife. As a kid I hated them, which I don't think was uncommon, and I only learned to love them when my wife or mother-in-law would roast their leaves until they were crispy. The first fried Brussels I ever ate were actually at a Mediterranean food truck parked outside a brewery. They were served sort of al dente with tahini sauce and I saw the potential in that flavor combination.

We began frying them at our pop-ups, this time whole until they were soft inside (almost creamy) and crispy outside. The Thick Tahini adds a nutty flavor and the salty brininess of the feta cuts against the richness perfectly. I've often joked that the most consistently raved about dish we make is the one we do the least too!

1 QUART CANOLA OIL, FOR FRYING

3 CUPS SMALL BRUSSELS SPROUTS

2 TABLESPOONS THICK TAHINI (SEE PAGE 108)

½ CUP FETA CHEESE

1 PINCH KOSHER SALT

1. Cut the bottoms off the sprouts, leaving them whole. If you only have large Brussel sprouts, halve them.

2. Heat the oil in a Dutch oven to approximately 350°F. Once the oil is to temperature, place the sprouts in the oil. Using a metal spoon, turn the sprouts every minute or so.

3. After approximately 4 minutes, or once the sprouts are golden brown, remove one from the oil and test for doneness. Finished Brussels sprouts should be able to be fully squeezed between your fingers (careful, they're hot; tongues work well for this test). Once the sprouts are all finished, remove them from the oil and shake them somewhat dry. A fry basket or strainer works for this step.

4. In a medium-sized bowl combine the sprouts, tahini, and feta well but carefully enough not to mush the sprouts. Sprinkle a pinch of salt and serve hot.

FRIED BRUSSELS SPROUTS WITH TAHINI & FETA, see page 93

SALATIM

Salatim. Veggie treatments. Starters. We call these unfamiliar to the American palate courses by a few different names. Essentially, a lot of the Israeli table consists of small, multi-step dishes meant to elevate vegetables to a space where they can be appreciated and serve to complement each other. Texture and color play big roles in these dishes; bright and crunchy, alongside deep and creamy. Spreads and salsas served with grilled or fried whole veggies. At Simcha we play up these differences and take liberties with the extremely varied ways in which our culture starts off the meal, and many of those dishes depend on the following recipes to serve as flavorful foundations.

PITA BREAD, see page 98

PITA BREAD

At its heart, Simcha is a restaurant built around this bread. We installed our centerpiece wood-fired oven specifically to produce fresh hot pita. In our culture pita is eaten with everything and we feel it is very important to make the best that we possibly can. It isn't as easy at home with your oven, but it is doable and the result is remarkable.

1 CUP LUKEWARM WATER

3 TEASPOONS DRY ACTIVE YEAST

3 TEASPOONS WHITE SUGAR

1¾ CUP ALL-PURPOSE WHITE FLOUR

1 CUP WHEAT FLOUR

1 TABLESPOON KOSHER SALT

1. In a large bowl combine the water, yeast, and sugar. Let sit for 15 minutes or so, until the water is foamy and bubbling. Add the flours and salt, mixing until the flour and water form a dough. Sprinkle with flour when necessary to work the dough. Knead the dough for 1 minute or so, just until the ball is smooth and uniform; it does not need to be kneaded otherwise. Set aside, covered by a towel or plastic wrap.

2. Preheat the oven to 500°F and place a cast-iron pan or upside-down baking sheet in the oven.

3. Separate the dough into 8 even pieces and ball them up. One at a time, on a floured surface, press the ball down and then, using a rolling pin, roll into a flat surface about ¼-inch thick.

4. Bake the pitas, 1 at a time. It will take approximately 3 minutes to puff up and 5 minutes or so to brown slightly and be done baking. Serve hot or keep at room temperature.

RED ZHOUG

My dad calls zhoug "Israeli ketchup" because he puts it on everything. To me, it's more like our Sriracha. It varies drastically, not only by the region, but even by the household. My take on it finds its way into numerous Simcha recipes.

4 FRESNO CHILES, STEMS REMOVED

2 CUPS PARSLEY

1 ONION, ROUGH CHOPPED

5 GARLIC CLOVES

JUICE OF 1 LEMON

1 TABLESPOON KOSHER SALT

1 TEASPOON CAYENNE

1 TABLESPOON CUMIN

2 TABLESPOONS PAPRIKA

¾ CUP EXTRA-VIRGIN OLIVE OIL

¼ CUP WATER, AS NEEDED

1. Cut the chilis into 5 pieces each. Place the chilis, parsley, onion, garlic, and lemon juice in a food processor and pulse until all of the ingredients are combined and rough chopped.

2. Add the salt, cayenne, cumin, paprika, and, while on high, slowly pour in the olive oil. If the mixture doesn't blend smoothly, add the water to help it along. The finished product should be smooth and a little pasty and will keep in the refrigerator for up to 2 weeks.

GREEN ZHOUG

Not only does this work as a stand-alone condiment, it makes for an outstanding marinade.

4 JALAPEÑOS, STEMS REMOVED

2 CUPS PARSLEY

¼ CUP CILANTRO

6 MINT LEAVES

1 ONION, ROUGH CHOPPED

5 GARLIC CLOVES

JUICE OF 1 LEMON

1 TABLESPOON KOSHER SALT

½ CUP EXTRA-VIRGIN OLIVE OIL

¼ CUP WATER

1. Cut the jalapeños into 5 pieces each. Place the peppers, parsley, cilantro, mint, onion, garlic and lemon juice into a food processor and pulse until all ingredients are combined and rough chopped.

2. Add the salt and, while on high, slowly pour in the olive oil. If the mixture doesn't blend smoothly, add the water to help it along. The finished product should be the texture of a chimichurri and it will keep in the refrigerator for up to 1 week.

SMOKED EGG AIOLI

Our Smoked Egg Aioli is a basic mayonnaise made from gently smoked egg yolks and astringent white vinegar for a little more pop. We serve it with our Couscous Arancini, but it is also a dipping sauce for items and replaces mayo in some slaws. I highly recommend keeping some in the fridge for sandwiches or even tuna.

2 EGG YOLKS

½ CUP WOOD CHIPS, FOR SMOKING

1 TABLESPOON WHITE VINEGAR

1 TEASPOON KOSHER SALT

1 CUP CANOLA OIL

1. Place the yolks in a metal bowl. Place the bowl in a deep baking pan. In a cast-iron skillet over high heat, get the wood chips hot and light them. Place the cast iron on a sheet pan also, next to the bowl, and cover the pan with foil. Allow the smoke to flavor the yolks for 20 minutes.

2. In a small bowl, combine the yolks and vinegar and gently break the yolks and allow them to sit for 5 minutes.

3. Add the salt and slowly drizzle the oil into the yolks as you beat them, using an electric hand mixer or immersion blender. The mixture will thicken. If it remains too thin, slowly add a little more oil. Refrigerate for up to 6 days.

ZA'ATAR WHIPPED FETA

Whipped feta is a backbone ingredient for us. We use it under savory proteins and inside filled appetizers. We spoon it onto salads and serve it with warm bread on its own. It's incredibly easy to make, and very versatile.

2 CUPS CRUMBLED FETA CHEESE

2 TABLESPOONS ZA'ATAR

¼ CUP EXTRA-VIRGIN OLIVE OIL

1 TEASPOON CRUSHED RED PEPPER

JUICE FROM ½ LEMON

1. Add the feta and za'atar to a food processor and puree. Slowly drizzle in the olive oil until the mixture begins to smooth out. Add the crushed red pepper and lemon juice. Refrigerate for up to 5 days.

ZA'TAR WHIPPED FETA, see page 103

YIELD: 4 CUPS   TOTAL TIME: 1 HOUR

PICKLED APPLESAUCE

Created for my smoked pork belly, this apple sauce is simple but has real depth. Essentially an apple agrodolce, it is sweet and sour and cuts against rich, fatty meats. It is versatile as a side, garnish, or condiment.

3 LBS. APPLES, PEELED AND SLICED (I USE GRANNY SMITH)

1 TEASPOON CINNAMON

1 PINCH CLOVE

½ CUP SUGAR

1½ CUPS WHITE VINEGAR

1. Combine all of the ingredients in a saucepan over high heat and bring to a boil. Once it is boiling turn down the heat to medium-high and simmer until reduced by one-third. Remove from heat and allow to cool to room temperature.

2. Mash the sauce by hand, or for best results put the mixture into a food processor for 2 minutes on high.

CARROT TOP ZHOUG

The two most common varieties of zhoug are green and red. When I can get my hands on the beautiful carrot greens a local farm near our restaurant grows, I like to use their vibrant flavor to create this spicy spread. It's an awesome way to use all of the vegetable and zhoug goes great, as my dad can attest to, on everything.

2 CARROT TOPS

3 JALAPEÑOS

¼ CUP CILANTRO

4 GARLIC CLOVES

½ CUP EXTRA-VIRGIN OLIVE OIL

4 MINT LEAVES

2 TEASPOONS KOSHER SALT

JUICE OF 1 LEMON

1. Add the carrot tops, jalapeños, cilantro, and garlic to a food processor and pulse. On high, drizzle in the oil, slowly creating a paste. Only add enough oil to create a tight paste. Add the mint, salt, and lemon juice, loosening the paste slightly.

2. Once it is fully blended, serve immediately or refrigerate; this condiment should keep for a week or so.

THICK TAHINI SAUCE

Thick tahini sauce is a staple of the traditional and modern Israeli kitchens. My father's generation grew up eating thick and creamy tahini (often pronounced *tahina* as a sauce) the way we eat hummus—with bread as a snack or as a condiment. This thick and creamy version is the base we use to start our Baba Ghanoush (see page 92) and it is also the secret to our very popular Brussels sprouts (see page 93). Thinned out with water it quickly becomes a delicious sauce to dress salads or top pita pockets with.

5 OZ. TAHINI

½ CUP WATER

3 GARLIC CLOVES

1 TEASPOON KOSHER SALT

JUICE OF 1 LEMON

1 PINCH CUMIN

1. Add the tahini and water to a food processor and pulse to combine. After 30 seconds add the garlic, salt, lemon juice, and cumin. Puree on high for 2 to 3 minutes, until the tahini is creamy and smooth.

ADLEY'S SAUCE

I learned how to cook starting when I was four. My dad taught me to smell, taste, and touch food. I watched food change by heat and by acid. I absorbed what it meant to create flavors. My 7-year-old son, Adley, has been in the kitchen since before he was two. Over the last few years, he has started making sauces. They're generally pretty bad, but he's learning and he's seeing. This sauce is a slight deviation from the first one he made, which was pretty tasty. I adjusted the texture and added a little acid, but we use it on chicken wings, pulled pork, even dip chicken nuggets in it. The ginger and paprika were a cool play, I learned something.

1 CUP WATER

1 TEASPOON KOSHER SALT

½ CUP WHITE VINEGAR

1 TEASPOON BLACK PEPPER

1 TABLESPOON PAPRIKA

1 TABLESPOON FRESH GINGER

½ CUP SUGAR

¼ CUP CORN SYRUP

1. Add all of the ingredients, except the cory syrup, to a saucepan over high heat and bring to a boil. Cook until the mixture reduces by one-third. Remove from heat, strain, and let cool.

2. Once it has cooled stir in the corn syrup for texture. Keeps in the refrigerator for up to a month.

YEMENITE HOT SAUCE

To me, cilantro is the key ingredient to this hot sauce, but if you are allergic or experience cilantro as soap, definitely omit it. Our Yemenite Hot Sauce is essentially a mix, in our minds, of our Red Zhoug's flavor profile and a Southern hot sauce meant to dip fried chicken in. I always have a jar of this on hand and use it, as the saying goes, on everything.

2 QUARTS WHITE VINEGAR

4 FRESNO CHILES, STEMS REMOVED

1 BUNCH OF CILANTRO, ROUGH CHOPPED

½ WHITE ONION, CHOPPED

4 GARLIC CLOVES

1 TEASPOON CUMIN

2 TEASPOOSN KOSHER SALT

2 TABLESPOONS CHICKEN FAT

1. Add the vinegar, chilis, cilantro, onion, garlic, cumin, and salt to a saucepan over high heat. Once the sauce begins to boil, reduce to medium heat and simmer for 45 minutes to an hour.

2. Remove from heat and pulse, using an immersion blender, food processor, or blender. Keep in mind the hot liquid will expand in a blender or food processor so be extremely careful if blending hot. It also works if you allow the ingredients to cool a bit. Use a strainer to separate the pulp from the sauce.

3. Add the chicken fat to a small saucepan over low heat, warm it through, and rigorously mix it into the sauce, creating a velvety texture.

YEMENITE HOT SAUCE, see page 111

MEYER LEMON MARMALADE

Spicy, sour, and sweet are flavor combinations that Israelis hold dear. Unlike amba—a fermented mango chutney—this marmalade is jammed and is never fermented. It's a universal condiment that can be used in all sorts of ways.

5 MEYER LEMONS

2 FRESNO CHILES, STEMS REMOVED AND DICED

4 GARLIC CLOVES, FINE DICED

1 TABLESPOON KOSHER SALT

1 TEASPOON BLACK PEPPER

1 CUP WATER

1 CUP WHITE VINEGAR

2 CUPS WHITE SUGAR

1. Cut the lemons, rind and all, into ½-inch chunks.

2. Add all of the ingredients to a saucepan over high heat. Once the mixture is boiling, reduce heat to medium-high and simmer for 45 minutes. Once everything has softened turn the heat back to high and reduce until the mixture reaches 220°F.

3. Remove from heat and allow to cool before transferring to containers for refrigeration; will keep refrigerated for up to a month.

SHAWARMA SPICE

Ras al-hanout means "the spice of the house" and varies from establishment to establishment throughout the Middle East. At Simcha, in tribute to our origins as a team working The Chubby Chickpea, we call our house spice Shawarma Spice because it was developed for our chicken shawarma. It is the base for many dishes: by adding sugar it becomes a rub, with a little vinegar and some chilis it transforms into a hot sauce.

½ **CUP PAPRIKA**

¼ **CUP GRANULATED GARLIC**

½ **CUP KOSHER SALT**

3 **TABLESPOONS BLACK PEPPER**

¼ **CUP CUMIN**

1 **TABLESPOON CINNAMON**

1 **TABLESPOON CAYENNE**

1 **TABLESPOON TURMERIC**

1 **TEASPOON CLOVE**

1. Combine all of the ingredients in a medium-sized bowl and mix well. Store in a dry place.

MOROCCAN SPICE

Our Moroccan spice loosely resembled pumpkin spice in its heavy use of warming spices. Unlike our house spice, we leave key savory ingredients (garlic, cumin) which are so pronounced throughout our menu out of our Moroccan spice. Turbinado sugar is something the pot master at a La Esh taught me to use, it cooks differently than white sugar. We use this spice in dishes such as our carrots, breads, sauces, fish.

2 TABLESPOONS TURBINADO SUGAR

¼ CUP PAPRIKA

1 TABLESPOON CLOVE

1 TABLESPOON NUTMEG

1 TABLESPOON CINNAMON

2 TABLESPOONS KOSHER SALT

1 TABLESPOON TURMERIC

1. Combine all of the ingredients in a medium-sized bowl and mix well. Store in a dry place.

SIMCHA'S MARINARA

I cringe when my cooks refer to my tomato sauce as marinara. To me, it's tomato sauce: it has cinnamon and cayenne, and is full of garlic. Initially, it's the sauce meant for our Albondigas (see page XXX). Over time I've given in and I just reason that it is our marinara, a house sauce if you will. We use it for spaghetti and meatballs on our takeout menu, and we eat it mixed into couscous mac at staff meal. It's a little different, just like us.

5 LARGE TOMATOES

½ CUP EXTRA-VIRGIN OLIVE OIL

1 LARGE ONION, JULIENNED

5 GARLIC CLOVES, MINCED

¼ CUP PARSLEY

1 TABLESPOON KOSHER SALT

1 TEASPOON CINNAMON

1 PINCH CAYENNE

1 TABLESPOON PAPRIKA

1 CUP WATER, AS NEEDED

1. Core each tomato and then cut each one into 8 pieces. Add all the tomato pieces to a bowl, making sure not to lose any juice.

2. Add the olive oil to a medium-sized saucepan over high heat. Once the oil is warmed through, add the onion and garlic. When the onions become translucent add the tomatoes and the remainder of the ingredients. If the tomatoes sweat enough, adding water won't be necessary, but there should always be liquid in the pan.

3. Cook over medium-high heat for 25 to 30 minutes, until all of the tomatoes can be mushed easily with a spoon and the sauce is fully incorporated.

4. Remove from heat. Use immediately or refrigerate for 3 to 5 days.

COUSCOUS ARANCINI

One of the many things we believe in as a team, hand-in-hand with supporting local farmers and butchers, is limiting food waste. Our couscous arancini comes from us needing a way to repurpose leftover couscous. I love them because like a lot of our menu items, they are familiar and yet completely different.

2½ CUPS WATER

2 CUPS COUSCOUS

1 TABLESPOON PAPRIKA

1 TABLESPOON GRANULATED GARLIC

2 TEASPOONS KOSHER SALT

1 TEASPOON CUMIN

1 CUP CRUMBLED FETA

CANOLA OIL, FOR FRYING

1. Bring the water to a boil.

2. In a medium-sized bowl, combine the couscous and the seasonings and mix well. Add the boiling water to the couscous and cover the bowl with plastic wrap. After 10 minutes use a fork to fluff the couscous. Add ½ cup feta to the couscous and mix well.

3. In a deep pot heat at least 4 inches of canola oil to 350°F.

4. Using your hands, ball up about 1 oz. couscous and, by pressing into the ball with your thumb, make a divot and fill it with feta and close the ball around it.

5. Once all of the couscous balls are formed and filled, fry them, 4 at a time, for approximately 4 minutes until they're golden brown. Serve hot.

SCALLOP CEVICHE

Ceviche, to me, embodies the feel and the spirit of modern-day Acre. A fishing city, Acre is unlike any other Israeli city and has a vibe that is more Greek Isles than Middle East. Fresh seafood is a hallmark of the city. Being a New Englander, I have loved fresh scallops in so many different recipes. This ceviche is crisp and fresh, like most Israeli salads, with tender scallop.

1 TEASPOON HONEY

½ TEASPOON POMEGRANATE MOLASSES

1 LIME, JUICED

1 SPLASH WHITE VINEGAR

1 PINCH KOSHER SALT

½ SHALLOT, DICED

1 TABLESPOON SLICED SCALLIONS

2 MINT LEAVES, CHOPPED

1 TEASPOON CHOPPED JALAPEÑO

6 LARGE SEA SCALLOPS

1. In a medium bowl mix the honey and molasses into the lime juice and white vinegar. Add the salt, shallot, scallions, mint, jalapeño, and pepper to the bowl, mix well, and set aside for 15 minutes.

2. Using a sharp knife, cut the scallops into ⅛-inch thick round slices. Once the marinade has sat, add the scallops to the bowl and gently mix. In a minute or two, the scallops will "cook" and turn fully white. Serve immediately.

SCALLOP CEVICHE, see page 121

TURMERIC GINGER COCKTAIL SHRIMP, see page 126

TURMERIC GINGER COCKTAIL SHRIMP

Be sure not to overcook the shrimp in this light, satisfying dish, which is enlivened by how well ginger and turmeric complement one another.

1½ LBS. SHRIMP

1 TABLESPOON FRESH GRATED GINGER

2 GARLIC CLOVES, MINCED

1 TABLESPOON FRESH GRATED TURMERIC

2 TABLESPOONS CHOPPED SCALLIONS

1 SHALLOT, MINCED

JUICE OF 1 LIME

1 TABLESPOON KOSHER SALT

1 TEASPOON HONEY

1 TABLESPOON EXTRA-VIRGIN OLIVE OIL

1. Peel the shrimp, leaving only the tail, and devein the shrimp. Set aside.

2. In a large bowl combine the remainder of the ingredients, mix well, and then add the peeled shrimp. Cover the bowl and refrigerate for at least 2 hours, and no more than 6 hours.

3. In a hot frying pan over medium-high heat, add the shrimp and the marinating liquid; it works best to do this in batches. Cook the shrimp until they have turned completely white/pink, or reach 120°F.

4. Serve room temperature or cold.

TUNA KIBBEH NAYEH

The traditional dish Kibbeh Nayeh was featured fairly heavily in my first run with the Simcha pop-up series. At the restaurant, we've showcased it from time to time. I've always felt confident that it works and guests enjoy it. During summer months our New England customers lean toward the ocean a bit and I found it was important to highlight high-quality local fish with ceviches and crudos. This dish was inspired by my love of herbaceous tuna ceviche and spicy tuna rolls. It eats like a salad or poke bowl, perfect for an appetizer or entrée.

1 CUP BULGUR WHEAT

8 OZ. TUNA, SUSHI-GRADE

2 BASIL LEAVES, CHIFFONADE

2 MINT LEAVES, CHIFFONADE

JUICE OF 1 LIME

JUICE OF 1 LEMON

1 TEASPOON KOSHER SALT

1 PINCH BLACK PEPPER

¼ CUP RED ONION, FINE DICE

2 TABLESPOONS SMOKED EGG AIOLI (SEE PAGE 102)

1 RIPE AVOCADO

2 CUPS SHREDDED PHYLLO DOUGH (OPTIONAL)

2 TABLESPOONS UNSALTED BUTTER (OPTIONAL)

1. Add the bulger wheat a small saucepan, cover with water, and cook for 15 to 20 minutes, or until tender. Strain and run under cold water until cool.

2. Using a sharp knife, cut slices of tuna and then dice it into ¼-inch chunks.

3. In a bowl, combine the herbs, citrus juices, salt, and black pepper and mix well. Stir in the tuna, covering as much as possible. Allow to sit for 5 minutes, then add the bulgur wheat, red onion, and the aioli.

4. Cut the avocado into ¼-inch chunks as well, then gently fold these into the mixture, breaking them up as little as possible.

5. The mixture can be served over lettuce wraps, on its own with chips, or in a bowl as a snack. At Simcha, we pan-fry shredded phyllo dough until it is golden brown, and serve the Kibbe spooned over the buttery pastry. To do this, warm a nonstick frying pan and melt the butter. Place 1 cup of the phyllo into the melted butter and use a spatula to flatten it into a pancake. Brown on both sides, approximately 1 minute per side. Repeat with the remainder of the phyllo. Serve warm with the cold Kibbe.

TUNA KIBBEH NAYEH, see page 127

FIRE-ROASTED OYSTERS

When I had Simcha's wood oven installed its main purpose was to make perfect, fluffy, memorable pita every night on demand (see page 98). Wanting to dive in fully, I selected the manufacturer's "wood only" option, making our oven the first they'd built with no gas assist. I really wanted to train myself to cook using wood fire, without training wheels. And I wanted my cooks to embrace this style as well. Once we mastered this skill, our pita was not only consistently praised but we were able to add small touches to our menu that otherwise may never have been found. A native New Englander, I have become accustomed to eating delicious oysters raw on the half shell with tasty sauces during a weeknight bar crawl or wedding cocktail hour. By roasting these bivalves in a fire there is a flavor and warmth (pardon the pun) achieved that make them so much more. These can also be cooked on a grill on under the broiler.

20 FRESH OYSTERS

3 TABLESPOONS UNSALTED BUTTER

½ CUP MINCED GARLIC

½ CUP GRATED PARMESAN CHEESE

¼ CUP CHOPPED PARSLEY

1. Rinse and shuck the oysters, making sure to separate them from their shell at the tendon.

2. Arrange the oysters in a cast-iron pan and put a small dollop of butter, a pinch of garlic, and a pinch of Parmesan into each oyster's shell.

3. On extremely high heat—we do these at 750-900°F, so as high as you can go—put the pan close to the fire. If using a grill, close the cover. The oysters are ready when the butter and cheese have turned golden brown, about 2 minutes.

4. Garnish with parsley and serve immediately.

POMEGRANATE MOLASSES MIGNONETTE

Pomegranate molasses imparts a sweet and savory quality to this sauce.

¾ CUP WHITE VINEGAR

1 TABLSPOON FINE DICED FRESNO CHILE

1 SHALLOT, SLICED THIN

1 TABLESPOON SLICED SCALLIONS

2 TABLESPOONS POMEGRANATE MOLASSES

1 TABLESPOON HONEY

1 TEASPOON KOSHER SALT

1. In a small saucepan on low heat warm your vinegar. Stir the molasses and honey in, mixing until dissolved. Add the salt and remove from heat. Allow to sit for 10 minutes or until slightly cooled and add chilis, shallots, and scallions. Steep in the refrigerator for a half-hour at least or up to 2 days.

2. Spoon onto raw oysters, making sure to get some of the chile, shallots, and scallions. Serve immediately.

SWORDFISH CRUDO, see page 136

SWORDFISH CRUDO

Often overlooked by "traditional" Middle Eastern cuisines is the region's proximity to the beauty of the sea. In Israel today, this has become a focal point, and contemporary Israeli cuisine has highlighted the ocean's bounty in ways our grandmothers never thought to. Rather than bury every fish in heavily spiced tomato sauce (obviously, as this book illustrates, those dishes are still delicious and still worthy), sometimes a more "Mediterranean" approach is used. To me, crudo marries perfectly the simplistic side of Israeli cooking with the light mezze style midday meals Israelis are famous for.

4 OZ. SUSHI-GRADE SWORDFISH

1 TEASPOON KOSHER SALT

1 TEASPOON FRESH CRACKED PEPPER

½ LEMON, SEEDED

1 TABLESPOON EXTRA-VIRGIN OLIVE OIL

1 TABLESPOON SLICED SCALLION

4 SLICES JALAPEÑO

3 SLICES FRESH TOMATO

1. Chill a plate in the refrigerator for 10 minutes.

2. Thinly slice the fish against the grain and arrange the slices on the chilled plate, making sure not to overlap the pieces.

3. Salt the fish generously, then crack the pepper over the fish, and then squeeze the lemon over the plate. Add the olive oil in the same fashion and sprinkle the scallion last.

4. Place the jalapeño and tomato on the side of the plate and serve cold.

ROASTED GRAPES & SAUSAGE

This simple oven-roasted salad contrasts salty, spicy sausage against almost overly sweet ripe grapes. Cooking them together imparts another layer of flavor, easily adding complexity without adding work. It's quick and lends itself to variations based on your flavor preferences or what you have on hand.

8 OZ. HUNGARIAN SAUSAGE

1 BUNCH MUSCAT GRAPES

3 OZ. FRESH MOZZARELLA, TORN

2 TABLESPOONS BALSAMIC REDUCTION

1. Preheat broiler to 500°F.

2. Slice the sausage into ¼-inch thick slices.

3. Place the sliced sausage and bunches of grapes in an oven-safe pan. Once the sausage is very browned and partially cupped, remove the pan from the oven and move the sausage and grapes to a serving platter.

4. Scatter the mozzarella over the sausage and grapes, drizzle the balsamic reduction over the plate, and serve warm.

ROASTED GRAPES & SAUSAGE, see page 137

SMOKED SWEET POTATO PUREE

Often eaten in spicy stews or pan-fried, sweet potatoes are a staple in Israeli cuisine and are typically used in much more savory preparations than those found in New England. At Simcha, we split the difference by making our creamy puree with a little bit of smoke. It's sweet and savory, and it has a depth of flavor that surprises first-time guests. We serve it underneath our fried chicken, but it can be served on its own as a satisfying side dish.

2 SWEET POTATOES, PEELED

1 WHITE POTATO, PEELED

½ CUP WOOD CHIPS, FOR SMOKING

2 TABLESPOONS UNSALTED BUTTER

2 TEASPOONS KOSHER SALT

½ CUP CREAM

1. Preheat the oven to 250°F.

2. Cut the sweet potatoes and the potatoes into 3-inch chunks. In a cast-iron pan over high heat, light your wood chips on fire. Place the cast-iron and the wood chips into a deep roasting pan. Add the potatoes next to – not on top of – the pan and cover the roasting pan with foil. Put the roasting pan into the oven for 30 minutes.

3. In a large pot, boil at least 10 cups of water. After 30 minutes remove the potatoes from the oven and boil them until they are soft enough to mash, about 25 minutes.

4. Strain fully and place the potatoes into a food processor with the butter, salt, and cream. Process until completely smooth.

5. Serve hot.

CHEESY POOFS

This amazing snack came about as a way to make sure our Smoked Sweet Potato Puree never goes to waste.

CANOLA OIL, FOR DEEP FRYING

2 CUPS SMOKED SWEET POTATO PUREE (PAGE 141)

1 EGG

½ CUP ALL-PURPOSE FLOUR

½ TEASPOON BAKING POWDER

¼ CUP GRATED ASIAGO CHEESE

¼ CUP GRATED PARMESAN CHEESE

⅓ CUP GRATED MOZZARELLA CHEESE

1. Add at least 4 inches of canola oil to a deep pot over medium-high heat and bring to 350°F.

2. Add the puree and egg to a bowl and mix well. Add the flour and baking powder, whisk until smooth, then fold in the cheeses.

3. Once the oil is ready for frying, drop tablespoon-size balls (an ice cream scooper works perfectly) into the oil. After one minute turn the poofs so they expand evenly on both sides. Fry for 4 minutes, until brown on all sides.

4. Serve hot.

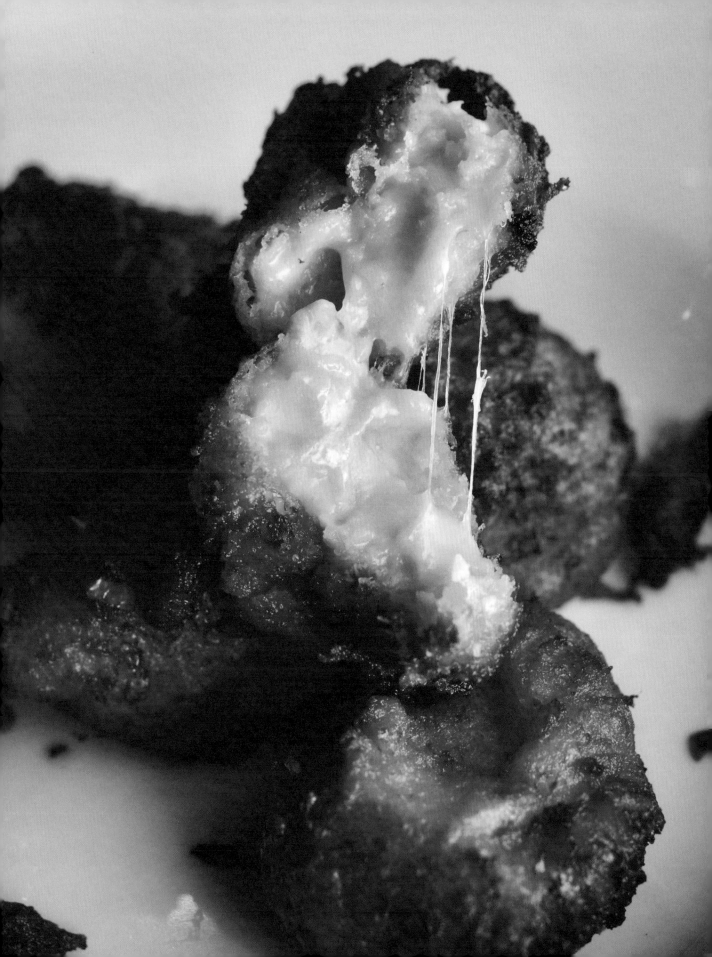

MARINATED LAMB HEART

The first animal that we started butchering in-house was lamb, and it was a real transition for me in the way I viewed animals and food waste. Feeling the weight of the still warm lamb when I left the slaughterhouse, I felt more committed than ever to use as much of the animal as possible. When Joe, our butcher, finished breaking the meat down I got a pan hot and seared the heart. We all shared the tender meat; it was a very communal end to a process that had begun much earlier. Aside from the desire not to waste food, lamb heart is tasty and tender—it eats very much like filet. This interesting and delicious meat is a beautiful complement to a creamy starch.

½ CUP WHITE VINEGAR

2 TABLESPOONS EXTRA-VIRGIN OLIVE OIL

¼ CUP CHOPPED PARSLEY

1 TEASPOON CORIANDER

½ WHITE ONION, MINCED

3 MINT LEAVES, CHOPPED

3 BASIL LEAVES, CHOPPED

2 GARLIC CLOVES, MINCED

2 TEASPOONS KOSHER SALT

1 (6-8 OZ.) LAMB HEART

1. Add all of the ingredients, except the lamb heart, to a bowl and mix well.

2. Place the lamb heart on a cutting board and use a sharp knife to remove the connective tissue—white with honeycomb-like texture—from the outside of the lamb heart. Place the heart in the marinade and refrigerate for 2 to 4 hours.

3. On a hot grill or in a very hot skillet, place the lamb heart top-side down. For medium-rare, after approximately 2 minutes turn over the lamb heart. After another 2 minutes, remove the lamb from the heat and allow to rest for a few minutes. For more well-done meat add a few minutes of cooking time for each side.

4. Slice the lamb heart into ½-inch slices and serve hot.

BRUNCH & BOOZE

I love our brunch service because brunch is the closest thing American cuisine has to the way we eat Mediterranean food, with shared tables full of food and rounds of drinks. These cocktails and indulgent breakfast foods help bridge the gap between the two worlds Simcha represents.

NDUJA SHAKSHUKA RECIPE

I fell in love with shakshuka on the beaches of Eilat. It became all I wanted to cook, but I couldn't make it fit into my food truck and catering business so I launched a pop-up brunch series at a friend's restaurant. Of course, that meant we'd have to make more than shakshuka. Simcha was born in these services, as we started playing with flavors and straddling comfort food and deep warm flavors.

½ CUP EXTRA-VIRGIN OLIVE OIL

8 GARLIC CLOVES

2 MEDIUM YELLOW ONIONS, DICED

6 OZ. NDUJA

6 TOMATOES, CUT INTO ⅛THS

1 TABLESPOON KOSHER SALT

1 TEASPOON FRESH CRACKED BLACK PEPPER

2 TEASPOONS GROUND CUMIN

1 TABLESPOON PAPRIKA

1 CHILE PEPPER, DICED (OPTIONAL)

6 LARGE EGGS

4 OZ. GOAT CHEESE

1 BUNCH FLAT PARSLEY, CHOPPED

1. In a food processor, combine olive oil and garlic.

2. Add the oil and garlic mixture to a large, deep frying pan over medium-high heat. After about 2 minutes, add onions, stirring slowly until they become translucent, approximately 3 to 4 minutes.

3. Add the nduja, stirring slowly with a wooden spoon every 30 seconds or so, allowing the meat to melt into the onions. After 2 minutes add the tomatoes and top with salt, pepper, cumin, paprika, and chile pepper, if using. Cover and allow to simmer for 15 minutes, stirring only slightly if it seems like the bottom may be burning. (If the tomatoes don't produce enough liquid to keep the bottom from burning, add water ¼ cup at a time).

4. After 15 minutes, stirring once or twice to help the tomatoes break down. Turn down heat to medium and allow to simmer for 10 more minutes.

5. Once the sauce is ready, distribute the goat cheese evenly across the surface. Distribute the eggs across the surface and put the lid back on. In about 2 to 3 minutes the eggs should be perfectly over easy. Sprinkle the parsley and serve.

PINTO BEAN FŪL, see page 152

PINTO BEAN FŪL

For true Middle Easterners, fūl is the classic brunch dish. Fava beans cooked down with onions and spices, smothered in tahini, and served with hard-boiled eggs make for the ultimate late-morning meal. I stay away from fava beans in my version and instead use pinto beans. Served with thick tahini, zhoug, and hard-boiled eggs this dish is a real treat.

16 OZ. DRIED PINTO BEANS

3 TABLESPOONS EXTRA-VIRGIN OLIVE OIL

3 GARLIC CLOVES, MINCED

1 WHITE ONION, DICED SMALL

1 TABLESPOON CUMIN

1 TEASPOON CAYENNE

1 TABLESPOON SALT

1 CUP WATER

TAHINI, TO SERVE

GREEN ZHOUG (SEE PAGE 101), TO SERVE

HARD-BOILED EGGS, TO SERVE

1. Soak the pinto beans overnight in cold water, making sure all of the beans are covered by at least 3 inches of water.

2. Drain the beans from the water and put them into a medium saucepan covered by at least 3 inches of water. Bring to a boil and cook for 45 minutes to an hour, or until the beans are soft enough to mash between your thumb and forefinger. Strain the beans and set aside.

3. Add the oil to a large frying pan over high heat. When the oil begins to shimmer add the garlic and onions. As the onions begin to sweat, add cumin, cayenne, and salt. After 5 minutes add the beans and stir regularly. Add the water ¼ cup at a time to keep the mixture from burning. Each time water begins to disappear at another ¼ cup.

4. After the entire cup has been used and there is no excess water in the pan remove it from the heat.

5. Serve hot with tahini, Green Zhoug, and hard-boiled eggs.

BAKED-BRIE BOUREKAS

Baked brie is a delicious appetizer to make any time by wrapping a brie wheel with puff pastry. Using the same flavors, at brunch we serve individual versions in the form of the Middle Eastern pastry boureka. For the jam, use whatever type you like, or have readily available. I like to go with something tart, and when we can we make a strawberry-black lime jam that works well in this recipe.

4 (5"X5") PUFF PASTRY SQUARES

8 OZ. BRIE CHEESE

4 OZ. JAM

1 EGG

1 TABLESPOON SESAME SEEDS (OPTIONAL)

1. Preheat the oven to 375°F.

2. On a well-floured surface, lay out the four puff pastry squares. Spoon 1 oz. of jam into the middle of each square. Cut the brie into 4 equal pieces and place each into the center of the squares.

3. Pull all 4 corners of the pastry squares to the center and pinch them together, then twist so that they resemble a coin purse. Once all four purses are assembled, crack the egg into a small bowl, whisk, and, using a pastry brush, brush each purse with egg. Sprinkle the sesame seeds, if using.

4. Place the four purses on a baking sheet and bake for 15 to 20 minutes, until golden brown. The brie will be oozy. Serve hot, but eat carefully.

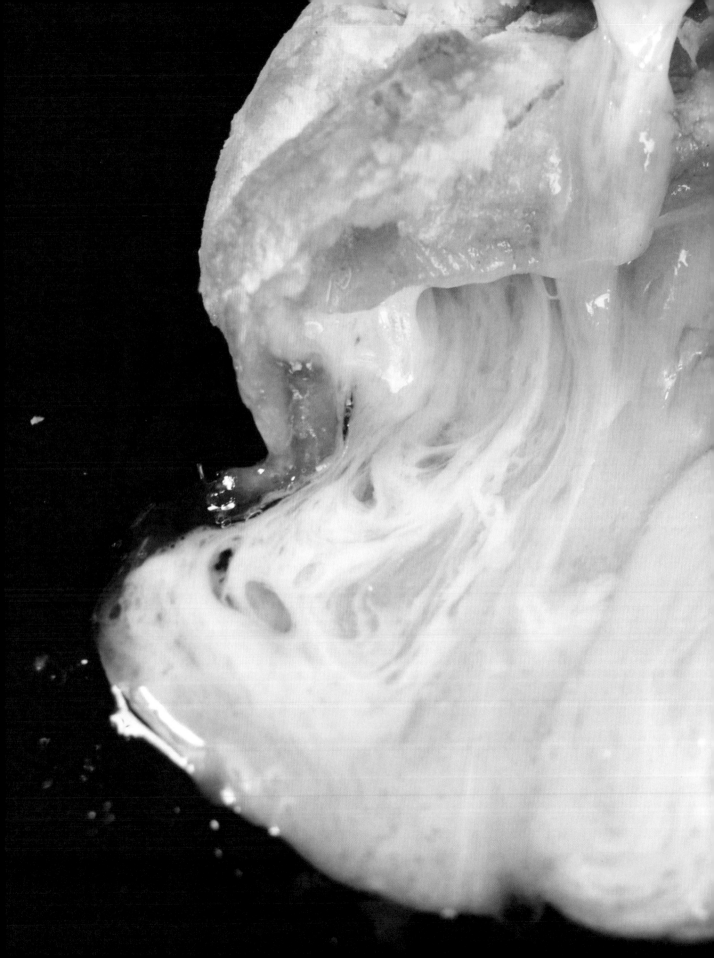

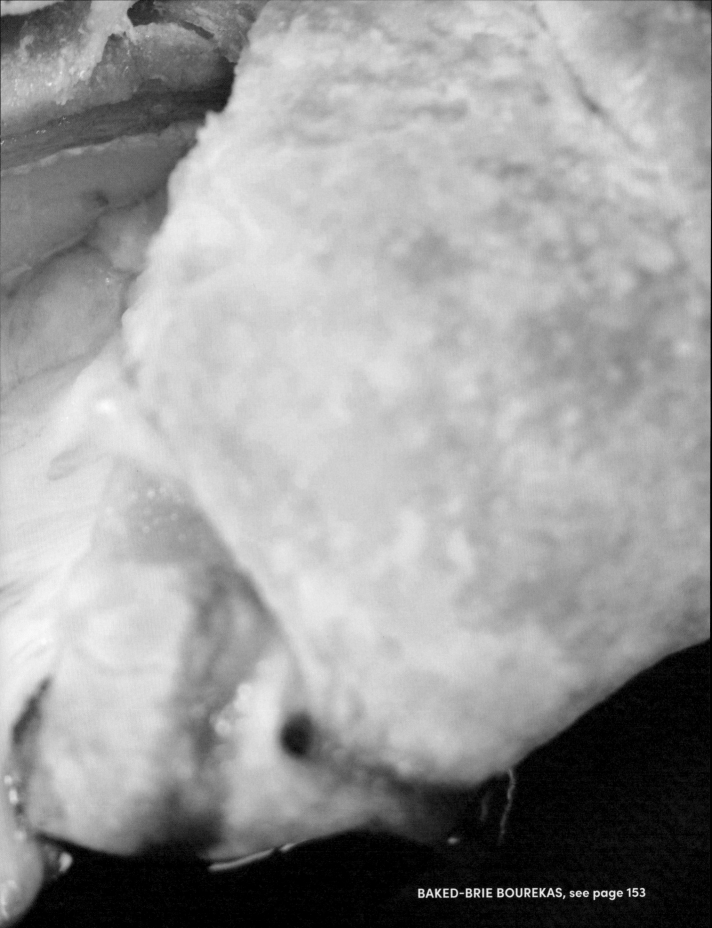

BAKED-BRIE BOUREKAS, see page 153

BACON & EGGS JACHNUN

Jachnun is a Yemenite dish, slowly cooked overnight so that it can be eaten warm in the morning, even on the Sabbath. In this preparation, we take advantage of the low-and-slow cooking method to also cook very tender, fall apart bacon. The eggs traditionally cooked alongside jachnun are called *huevos haminados*, or "slow-cooked eggs." They brown and caramelize in their shell. Once you master the technique of this overnight bread, you'll find this to be a rewarding and fun breakfast!

3¼ CUPS ALL-PURPOSE FLOUR

1½ CUPS WATER

1 TEASPOON BAKING POWDER

½ CUP UNSALTED BUTTER, MELTED

16 STRIPS OF BACON

8 EGGS

1. Preheat the oven to 210°F.

2. In a medium bowl, or using a stand mixer, combine the flour, water, and baking powder. Knead by hand or with the dough hook for 5 minutes, until a smooth, springy dough ball has formed. Cover with a tea towel and let the dough rest for 10 minutes.

3. Split the dough into 8 even-sized balls. Using a rolling pin on a well-floured surface, roll out each ball into as close to a rectangle as possible, and as thin as possible. Be gentle so the dough doesn't rip (a few small rips are fine). A trick I use is coating the dough in the butter before rolling it out. It's messy, but it saves a lot of time and makes the rolling process easier.

4. Once the rectangles have been formed and are as thin as possible, make sure they are thoroughly buttered. Apply butter to the surface using a pastry brush if necessary. Place two raw bacon strips an inch or so apart headed in the same direction as the dough (the long way).

5. Fold in the sides of the wide edge by an inch on both the top and bottom. Fold in the narrow edge by about 2 inches, then again over itself, and again until it's fully wrapped up. You should end up with a rolled-up dough that looks like a crescent roll. Repeat for all 8 rectangles.

6. Once the dough balls are all rolled up, place them tightly against each other in a baking pan. I prefer a circular pan, and I spiral them, but any baking pan will do. They must be packed tightly so they hold their shape as they cook. I don't put anything underneath them, but you can use parchment paper or stale bread if you want to.

7. Place the eggs, whole, into the pan on top of the dough balls. Cover the pan with foil and put the pan in the oven.

8. Bake for 8 to 10 hours. Remove from the oven and serve everyone one dough ball and one egg. Optional accompaniments include fresh salsa, zhoug, sour cream, and Pickled Applesauce (see page 106).

FRIED & STUFFED FRENCH TOAST, see page 160

FRIED & STUFFED FRENCH TOAST

When we started Simcha's pop-up series 4 years ago we knew brunch would be an important aspect. Centered around shakshuka, we wanted to build service that would be fun and innovative, featuring creative dishes alongside the traditional stuff. Matt Jones, the sous chef who worked brunch, showed me how he fried stuffed French toast and it's been a sweet staple ever since. Use whatever jam you prefer – we switch it up all the time.

2 CUPS CANOLA OIL, FOR FRYING

2 EGGS

3 TABLESPOONS JAM OF YOUR PREFERENCE

3 TABLESPOONS CREAM CHEESE

4 SLICES CHALLAH, 1"-THICK

CONFECTIONERS' SUGAR, TO SERVE (OPTIONAL)

SYRUP, TO SERVE (OPTIONAL)

1. Add canola oil to a medium-sized saucepan over medium-high heat.

2. Whisk the eggs in a bowl big enough to dip the bread slices.

3. In a small bowl, combine the jam and the cream cheese. Spoon this filling in the center of two challah slices and spread toward the edges, leaving an inch from all sides.

4. Put the second slice of challah on each piece with a filling, making a sandwich. Once the oil is hot enough, dip the sandwiches fully in the egg wash, coating on all sides. Place into the hot oil. The egg wash will seal the sandwich and prevent the filling from leaking. Allow the toast to brown on the first side for 2½ to 3 minutes, then flip it over and allow to brown for 2½ to 3 minutes on the second side.

5. Set the French toast on a cooling rack to remove any excess oil.

6. To serve, place the toast on a plate and cut it in half diagonally, allowing the filling to ooze out a little.

YIELD: 6 SERVINGS   **TOTAL TIME:** 12 HOURS

LAMB BELLY HASH

My food truck and catering company, The Chubby Chickpea, was certified Kosher for a short time. Trying to find a replacement for pork belly led me to lamb breast or lamb belly. It is a delicious and fatty cut, beautiful braised or smoked. This hash is an out-of-this world illustration of how good lamb belly is.

1 (12 OZ.) LAMB BREAST

2 TEASPOONS BLACK PEPPER

1 TEASPOON KOSHER SALT

APPLEWOOD SMOKING CHIPS

2 WHOLE POTATOES, SKIN ON

2 TABLESPOONS TRUFFLE OIL

3 GARLIC CLOVES, MINCED

1. Preheat the oven to 250°F.

2. Season the lamb with black pepper and salt and place it in a baking pan. Pour in 2 inches of water. Cover the pan with foil and place it in the oven. Braise for 8 hours.

3. In a smoker, or a covered stovetop pan, smoke the raw potatoes for 2 hours. Then boil the potatoes whole for 30 to 35 minutes, or until fork-tender. Set aside to cool.

4. Once the lamb has been braised and the potatoes are cooked, heat a large cast-iron skillet over high heat. Add the truffle oil and garlic to the pan. Next add the potatoes, mashing them with a spoon or spatula so that they flatten a bit and somewhat break apart. Add the lamb, trying to keep as little of the excess fat from the pan as possible.

5. Maintaining high heat, continue to break up the potato and lamb as they crisp up. The goal is to have evenly distributed lamb, potatoes, and garlic. Once everything is incorporated, about 5 to 7 minutes, turn down to medium heat and crisp the hash on both sides. Serve hot.

LOOKS LIKE AN IPA

Being a New England restaurant we're very familiar with IPAs that resemble bombs of pulpy orange juice. This cocktail is its own breed of hazy!

1 OZ. BOURBON

1 OZ. RYE

½ OZ. DRY VERMOUTH

¼ OZ. MARASCHINO CHERRY LIQUOR

¾ OZ. FRESH-SQUEEZED ORANGE JUICE

1. Combine all of the ingredients in a cocktail shaker and shake vigorously.

2. Add ice, shake again, and double strain into a cocktail glass.

SATURDAY AFTERNOON AFTER THE FARMERS MARKET

The fresh basil and local honey in this cocktail, combined with the airiness of the egg white foam, conjure up the happy feelings associated with a Saturday afternoon off. When my kids were super young, I used to take Saturday evenings off and we'd spend the morning grabbing fresh goodies from a local farmers market. The afternoon would be spent cooking, creating, and drinking a few cocktails.

4 BASIL LEAVES

½ OZ. HONEY

½ OZ. FRESH LEMON JUICE

1 OZ. GIN

1 OZ. SHERRY

1 EGG WHITE

1. Add the basil and honey to a cocktail shaker and muddle, then add the lemon juice and mix.

2. Add the gin and sherry and dry shake, then add ice and egg white, shake vigorously, and double strain into a cocktail glass.

LIMONANA

After the Arak Sour, this is our most traditional Israeli beverage. Limonana is so beautiful, an almost neon shade of green. It is also so refreshing. Very simple to make, and definitely a classic.

1½ OZ. VODKA

8 OZ. WATER

¼ CUP SUGAR

4 MINT LEAVES

2 OZ. FRESH LEMON JUICE

1 CUP ICE

1. In a blender combine all of the ingredients with 1 cup crushed ice, blend, and pour.

HEAT IN THE KITCHEN

I drink a ton of these at the beach. Super easy to drink, maybe too easy. If you've never had Fernet, it's herb forward, so this cocktail has a real "what is that flavor" thing going on while still being kind of a juicy punch.

1 OZ. GIN

1 OZ. FERNET

1½ OZ. LEMONADE

¼ OZ. GRENADINE

½ OZ. SELTZER

JUICE FROM 1 WHOLE ORANGE

ORANGE WEDGE, TO GARNISH

1. Combine all of the ingredients, except the seltzer, in a cocktail shaker with ice, shake vigorously, and strain over ice into a highball glass.

2. Top with seltzer and garnish with the orange wedge.

WHEN CHRISTMAS MISSED US

There's something nostalgic about the flavor combination of creamy orange. As lifelong underdogs, the feelings brought up by this tasty treat tie in with the triumphant vibes of B.I.G.'s juicy.

1 OZ. BLOOD ORANGE LIMONCELLO

1 OZ. RYE

¼ OZ. SIMPLE SYRUP

½ OZ. COINTREAU

SPLASH OF SODA

1. Combine all of the ingredients, except the soda, in a cocktail shaker with ice, shake vigorously, and double strain into a cocktail glass. Top with a splash of soda.

   BLOOD ORANGE LIMONCELLO: In an airtight container, combine 16 oz. American vodka and peels of 5 lemons and store at room temperature for 2 weeks. After the 2 weeks have passed, combine 2 cups sugar, 4 oz. fresh blood orange juice, and 12 oz. water in a small saucepan over medium heat and cook until the sugar dissolves, then bring the mixture to a boil and cook until it reaches 240°F. Remove from heat and set aside to cool. Add the syrup to the infused vodka, mix well, strain, and store in a sealed container in the refrigerator until cold.

TRIPLE MY WORTH

Tequila and arak became our thing at Simcha for a while. They're such distinct flavors and they play off each other very well. The cardamom syrup in this one is a little sweet, but it also brings an earthiness that balances the arak and tequila. The name is a play on Jay-Z's famous lyrics "put me anywhere on G-d's green earth and I'll triple my worth." Plus, this one will make you feel like you can do anything.

1½ OZ. TEQUILA

1 OZ. ARAK

¼ OZ. CARDAMOM SIMPLE SYRUP

¼ OZ. FRESH LIME JUICE

1. Combine all of the ingredients in a cocktail shaker with ice, shake vigorously, and strain over ice into a stemless wine glass.

PICKLED APPLESAUCE

A play off of our popular condiment, the lime and calvados play off each other here for a subtle and juicy combo.

1½ OZ. SPICED RUM

1 OZ. COINTREAU

½ OZ. CALVADOS

¼ OZ. SIMPLE SYRUP

½ OZ. FRESH LIME JUICE

1. Combine all of the ingredients in a cocktail shaker with ice, shake vigorously, and double strain over ice into a cocktail glass.

3 HOURS FROM HEATHROW

Strange trip. That's the vibe of this cocktail. More than a decade ago my wife and I were on our way to Israel when, about 30 minutes away from Heathrow for a connection, the tracker suddenly said 3 hours to Heathrow. Turns out the weather was rerouting us to Iceland, where we spent 36 hours in a dark, somewhat hazy state. Citrus, herb, spice, heat. This cocktail is as tasty as it is interesting.

2 OZ. CAPTAIN MORGAN SPICED RUM

1 OZ. FRESH LIME JUICE

½ OZ. JALAPEÑO SIMPLE SYRUP

2 DROPS MINT TINCTURE

1 OZ. TONIC WATER

1. Combine the rum, lime juice, and simple syrup in a cocktail shaker with ice and shake.

2. Add the mint tincture and tonic to the shaker and pour into a glass.

THE NIGHT
I GOT ENGAGED

The best night of my life. That's what this cocktail reminds me of. The ginger beer brings a champagne floater-like finish.

1 OZ. CALVADOS

1 OZ. RYE

½ OZ. FRESH LIME JUICE

¼ OZ. SIMPLE SYRUP

3 DROPS ANGOSTURA BITTERS

1 OZ. GINGER BEER

1. Combine all of the ingredients, except the ginger beer, in a cocktail shaker with ice, shake vigorously, and pour into a highball glass.

2. Top with ginger beer.

ISRAELI ICED TEA

Our take on the popular Long Island, this drink moves in the summer. Adding anise-based arak seems simple, but it drastically changes the cocktail into a flavorful and herbaceous drink.

1½ OZ. ARAK

¼ OZ. GIN

¼ OZ. TEQUILA

¼ OZ. VODKA

¼ OZ. TRIPLE SEC

JUICE OF 1 WHOLE LEMON

COCA-COLA, TO FILL

LEMON WEDGE, TO GARNISH

1. Combine all of the ingredients, except the Coca-Cola, in a glass, add ice, and then fill up the rest of the glass with the Coca-Cola.

2. Gently transfer into a shaker and then back into the glass and garnish with the lemon wedge.

BOSTON TEA PARTY

For most of my 20s, I would make terrible cocktails at home and call them all The Boston Tea Party. This one was born when we started making the Maker's Mark Baklava. We had so much bourbon coming and going I knew we needed to find an easy drinker to mix it into. Brown sugar lemonade is just different enough that this one quickly became our top cocktail.

1½ OZ. BOURBON

BROWN SUGAR LEMONADE

LEMON WEDGE, TO GARNISH

1. Add ice to an Old Fashioned glass, then add the bourbon and fill up the rest of the glass with the lemonade. Garnish with the lemon wedge.

   BROWN SUGAR LEMONADE: In a large bowl, combine 5 cups water, 1 cup fresh lemon juice, and 1 cup water and whisk until the sugar has fully dissolved.

FROZEN WHITE SANGRIA

In the summer we keep a frozen drink machine rolling all afternoon and evening! This drink is the brainchild of our GM Chris Riegel, but I promise I've had the most of them!

2 OZ. PINOT GRIGIO

2 OZ. WHITE PEACH JUICE

1 OZ. PEACHTREE SCHNAPPS

¼ OZ. BLACKBERRY BRANDY

JUICE OF 1 LIME

1. In a blender combine all of the ingredients with 1 cup crushed ice, blend, and pour.

ARAK SOUR

Simcha's take on Israel's working man's cocktail.

1½ OZ. ARAK

1½ OZ. SIMPLE SYRUP

½ OZ. FRESH LIME JUICE

½ OZ. GRAPEFRUIT JUICE

LIME WEDGE, TO GARNISH

1. Combine all of the ingredients in a cocktail shaker with ice, shake vigorously, pour into a highball glass, and garnish with the lime wedge.

ENTREES

As part of the evolution of Israeli cuisine on this side of the world, it's been important to use techniques and flavors familiar to Mediteranean cuisine and introduce them to more Western protein-centric preparations. We want to push forward, and so kebabs and grilled meats could never represent us fully. A very important characteristic of many of our entrees though is that they mirror our small plates; they're experiences and easily shared. You don't eat them simply for nourishment. Whole fish, stews, fried half-chicken—these are what have come to define our main courses.

SUMAC & LIME MAHI-MAHI, see page 184

SUMAC & LIME MAHI-MAHI
WITH PICKLED APPLE COUSCOUS

Mahi-mahi is such a tender, gently flavored fish and it takes marinades very well. This preparation is bright and warm, pairing beautifully with the subtle flavors in the couscous.

JUICE OF 2 LIMES

1 TABLESPOON SUMAC

1 TEASPOON HONEY

2 TEASPOONS KOSHER SALT, DIVIDED

1 GARLIC CLOVE, MINCED

2 (6 OZ.) MAHI-MAHI FILLETS

2 TABLESPOONS EXTRA-VIRGIN OLIVE OIL, DIVIDED

½ WHITE ONION, DICED

¼ CUP CHOPPED PARSLEY

1 TABLESPOON CHOPPED MINT

1 TABLESPOON CHOPPED CILANTRO

1 TABLESPOON CHOPPED BASIL

1 CUP COUSCOUS

1 CUP BOILING WATER

1. In a small bowl, whisk together the lime juice, sumac, honey, 1 teaspoon salt, and garlic. Add the mahi-mahi and refrigerate for at least 2 hours.

2. Add 1 tablespoon of olive oil to a frying pan over medium heat, and when warm add onion and the remainder of the salt. Stir in the parsley, mint, cilantro, and basil and remove from heat.

3. In a medium-sized bowl thoroughly mix these ingredients with the couscous. Pour in the boiling water and cover the bowl with plastic wrap. After 10 minutes remove the plastic wrap and, using a fork, fluff the couscous. Set aside.

4. Add the remainder of the olive oil to a small frying pan over medium heat. When the oil begins to shimmer, add the mahi-mahi, bottom-side down. Let the fish cook on that side for 4 to 5 minutes, and then turn it over, allowing the second side to also cook for 4 to 5 minutes. Once the fish easily flakes apart (or is 145°F) it is done.

5. Serve on top of the couscous.

CLAM CHOWDER TAHDIG

Here is another New England spin on tahdig, a traditional communal dish.

¼ **CUP EXTRA-VIRGIN OLIVE OIL**

1 **PINCH SAFFRON**

1 **WHITE ONION, DICED**

2 **GARLIC CLOVES, MINCED**

1 **TEASPOON KOSHER SALT**

1 **TEASPOON BLACK PEPPER**

¼ **CUP SMALL DICED UNCURED BACON**

1 **CUP FRESH COOKED CLAMS**

2 **TABLESPOONS ALL-PURPOSE FLOUR**

2 **CUPS WHOLE MILK**

½ **CUP CREAM**

1 **CUP BASMATI RICE**

½ **CUP SOUR CREAM**

1. Add the olive oil to a large frying pan over high heat. After 2 to 3 minutes, add the saffron and then the onions, garlic, salt, and pepper. Stir often until the onions are translucent. Remove half of the onions and put them aside for the rice mixture.

2. Add the bacon and clams to the pan and stir gently for 1 minute. Sprinkle flour over the mixture and stir to combine, creating a paste. Slowly add milk and cream, ¼ cup at a time, mixing thoroughly to avoid clumps. Once the milk and cream are incorporated, reduce the heat to medium and simmer; it will thicken as it cooks.

3. In a large pot, bring at least 5 cups of water to a boil and then add the rice. Boil rice for 15 to 20 minutes, until tender, and then strain.

4. In a small saucepot, combine the rice with the onion mixture and sour cream.

5. Place the saucepot over medium-high heat and cook the mixture, without stirring, until the edges crisp, about 7 minutes. Remove from heat and turn upside down on a flat plate.

6. To serve, ladle the chowder on top of the crisped rice.

CLAM CHOWDER TAHDIG, see page 185

ZHOUG MARINATED GRILLED SWORDFISH, see page 190

ZHOUG MARINATED GRILLED SWORDFISH
OVER PICKLED FRUIT SALAD

There's a lot to love about this grilled swordfish. The fish absorbs so much of the herbaceous and spicy zhoug. The fruit salad is fresh and zesty. The goat's milk feta is sweet and salty. This is an elegant and exciting summer meal.

8 OZ. SWORDFISH STEAK

½ CUP GREEN ZHOUG (SEE PAGE 101)

¼ CUP BLACKBERRIES

¼ CUP CHUNKED APPLES

¼ CUP QUARTERED STRAWBERRIES

¼ CUP CHUNKED PEARS

1 TEASPOON CHOPPED DILL

1 TEASPOON CHOPPED MINT

2 TEASPOONS KOSHER SALT, DIVIDED

1 TEASPOON SUGAR

¼ CUP WHITE VINEGAR

1 TEASPOON MAYONNAISE

1 TEASPOON CRACKED BLACK PEPPER

2 OZ. GOAT'S MILK FETA CHEESE

1. Fully coat both sides of the swordfish with zhoug, place in a container with a lid, and refrigerate overnight.

2. Heat the grill to high.

3. In a small bowl combine the fruit, herbs, 1 teaspoon salt, sugar, and vinegar and mix well. Set aside.

4. Remove the zhoug from the swordfish and coat the swordfish on both sides with mayonnaise and season with remaining salt and black pepper.

5. Place the swordfish on the grill and let the first side cook for 6 minutes. Flip the fish and let the second side go for 4 to 6 minutes, or until the fish is white and flaky all the way through (or 145°F).

6. To serve, pile the fruit salad in a shallow bowl or plate with a rim. Place the feta on top of the salad and lean the fish on top of the cheese.

SMOKED PORK BELLY IN PICKLED APPLESAUCE

Traditionally pork belly is smoked for a short time and then braised, after which it is pressed. It becomes a delicious little brick of smoky pork fat. By smoking the belly all the way through, the flavors are richer, and the texture is more in line with the fattiest flavor nuggets at the edge of a brisket. Our popular Pickled Applesauce condiment cuts against these indulgences and provides a very ying-yang eating experience.

6 OZ. CENTER-CUT PORK BELLY

½ CUP SHAWARMA SPICE (SEE PAGE 115)

3 TEASPOONS BROWN SUGAR

½ CUP PICKLED APPLESAUCE (SEE PAGE 106)

APPLEWOOD CHIPS

1. Set your smoker to 225°F.

2. In a small bowl, combine the Shawarma Spice and brown sugar and mix well. Fully coat the pork with this rub and place it, fat-side up, on a rack inside the smoker. Smoke for 10 hours, making sure the first 2 hours are on smoke.

3. Before removing the belly from the smoker, pour the Pickled Applesauce into a shallow bowl. Carefully move the belly into the center of the dish. Serve hot.

SMOKED PORK BELLY IN PICKLED APPLESAUCE, see page 191

STUFFED ACORN SQUASH, see page 196

STUFFED ACORN SQUASH

Kyle Crusius, who started as my sous chef at The Chubby Chickpea, became the executive chef of that kitchen and has run the Simcha kitchen since early 2020. He developed this recipe. The split peas make me think of soup my father would make when I was a kid, and with the squash this makes for a perfect vegetarian entree. All in all, this dish is pretty and hearty, not to mention delicious.

1 ACORN SQUASH

2 TABLESPOONS MOLASSES

1 TABLESPOON SALT, DIVIDED

CANOLA OIL

½ CUP BASMATI RICE

1 TEASPOON CINNAMON

½ TEASPOON CLOVE

½ TEASPOON NUTMEG

1 PINCH CAYENNE

1 TABLESPOON UNSALTED BUTTER

¼ CUP SPLIT PEAS

1. Preheat the oven to 425°F.

2. Remove the top and seeds from the squash and set aside the seeds.

3. Rub molasses into the cavity of the squash and sprinkle with half of the salt. Rub the outside of the squash with canola oil. Roast the squash upside down on a sheet pan until tender, approximately 40 minutes.

4. Clean, rinse, and dry the seeds. Place them on a separate sheet pan and roast until golden brown, about 20 minutes.

5. In a large pot boil 3 cups of water. In a smaller pot boil 2 cups of water.

6. Once the water boils, cook the rice in the larger pot with the remaining seasoning, boiling until tender, about 15 minutes. Strain and set aside.

7. Boil the split peas in the smaller pot for 30 minutes. When they are done strain and then add the peas to the rice.

8. Stuff the squash with rice mixture and garnish with roasted seeds.

ZA'ATAR-CRUSTED BEEF RIB EYE

This recipe is all about treating the meat properly. This starts with removing excess fat, which if left on the steak will get in the way of developing a crust. You also want to be sure not to under season the meat. Remember, you can't season the inside of a steak so the outside needs to make up for that.

2½ OZ. RIB EYE STEAK, AT ROOM TEMPERATURE

1 TABLESPOON CRACKED BLACK PEPPER

2 TEASPOONS KOSHER SALT

1 TEASPOON DRY THYME

1 TEASPOON SUMAC

1 TEASPOON WHITE SESAME

1. Heat up the grill. If cooking with gas, leave a burner on medium for the steak to transfer to; if cooking with wood or charcoal leave space where the flame will be less hot.

2. Trim any exterior fat or connective tissue from the steak.

3. Right before placing the meat on the grill combine all of the seasoning in a small bowl, mix well, and generously season the steak on all sides.

4. Place the steak on the grill and leave it, untouched, for 3 minutes. Check to see that the steak is developing a nice crust and getting good, deep markings. Turn the steak over, in the exact same spot facing the exact same way and cook for another 3 minutes.

5. After the steak has cooked on both sides and developed some crust and markings, turn it back over, this time placing it on the less hot section of the grill. Turn it over and turn 45° so that the lines from the grill will intersect to form diamonds. After 2 to 3 minutes on the grill turn the steak over, again matching the direction and position you have just turned it from. After 2 to 3 more minutes remove from heat. The steak should be around 130°F when you remove it, for medium rare. If aiming for a more done steak, add a minute to each step rather than adding more cook time to just one step.

6. Rest the steak for at least 5 minutes before slicing and serving.

ZA'ATAR-CRUSTED BEEF RIB EYE, see page 197

WHOLE BRANZINO, see page 202

WHOLE BRANZINO

Pan-roasted whole fish is completely about technique and patience, rather than about ingredients. Fresh fish is no doubt the major component, but after that, it is a show of cooking expertise rather than a simple mixing of ingredients. Similarly, ordering and eating whole fish requires its own sort of expertise. The fat content of branzino, often called "fatty bass," provides a lot of leeway when cooking. I much prefer this fish crisped up in a pan rather than grilled, as doing it this way steams the meat perfectly.

1 (1-2 LBS.) WHOLE BRANZINO

1 TABLESPOON KOSHER SALT

1 TABLESPOON FRESH CRACKED BLACK PEPPER

2 LEAVES FRESH BASIL

2 TABLESPOONS EXTRA-VIRGIN OLIVE OIL

½ LEMON

1. Preheat the oven to 425°F.

2. After the fish has been cleaned and scaled, pat dry using paper towels. Rub the fish with basil leaves and evenly distribute the salt and pepper on both sides.

3. Add the olive oil to a large cast-iron pan over high heat. When the oil begins to shimmer swirl it around in the pan. Set the fish in the coated pan and allow to brown on one side, approximately 4 to 5 minutes, and then turn and repeat for another 4 to 5 minutes.
   Place the pan in the oven and roast the fish for about 10 minutes, or until it registers an internal temperatures of 145°F.

4. Once the fish is out of the oven, use a spatula to place it onto a plate. Squeeze the lemon over the top and serve hot.

GARLIC CLAMS & PAPPARDELLE

People often ask me when they see items like clams, squid, or pork on my menus whether my grandmother would have eaten those items. Their point is well understood, but my response, which I genuinely believe to be true, is that if she were alive in present-day America she would. At her core, my grandmother was a provider, a nourisher, and a cook who drew big flavors from inexpensive sources. Clams add so much flavor to a dish like this one, which otherwise is a simple but beautiful summery tomato sauce. I'm certain that not only would she eat this pasta, but I believe she would thoroughly enjoy it.

¼ **EXTRA-VIRGIN OLIVE OIL**

½ **WHITE ONION, JULIENNED**

4 GARLIC CLOVES, MINCED

1 PINT GRAPE TOMATOES

1 TEASPOON FRESH CRACKED BLACK PEPPER

2 TEASPOONS KOSHER SALT, DIVIDED

4 OZ. CLAMS, FRESH IN SHELL

6 OZ. PAPPARDELLE

¼ **CUP CHOPPED PARSLEY**

1. Bring a large pot of water to a boil.

2. Add the olive oil to a large frying pan over high heat. When the oil begins to shimmer add the onions and garlic, stirring frequently until the onions become translucent. Add the tomatoes, pepper, and 1 teaspoon salt. Allow the tomatoes to break down for 5 minutes and then add the clams and cover the pan.

3. Add 1 teaspoon of salt to the boiling water along with the pasta. If using fresh pasta, cook for 4 to 5 minutes; if using dried pasta, cook for 10 to 12 minutes.

4. After 4 or 5 minutes check if all of the clams have opened up. If they haven't, cover and check every minute.

5. When the pasta is finished, use tongs to add the pasta to the pan with the clams and sauce. Stir in the parsley, toss lightly, and serve.

GARLIC CLAMS & PAPPARDELLE, see page 203

YIELD: 2 SERVINGS   **TOTAL TIME**: 30 MINUTES

DUCK BREAST WELLINGTON

Along the journey to opening Simcha, we did one service at a Boston-area restaurant known for hosting new concepts. For the occasion, me and my sous chef Andy Gregory came up with this dish. Baking the puff pastry while nailing the under the aspect of the duck was meant to be a show of skill, while the crispy duck skin and zesty feta made for an explosive flavor combo. Serve the dough pocket intentionally skin side down so as your guest cuts they can easily penetrate the duck and skin.

1 DUCK BREAST, SKIN ON

1 (5" X 5") PUFF PASTRY SQUARE

1 TABLESPOON ZAATAR WHIPPED FETA (SEE PAGE 103)

1. Warm a cast-iron skillet over medium-high heat.

2. Score the skin of the duck breast by using a sharp knife to cut a diamond pattern deep enough to almost reach the meat.

3. Once the pan has heated up, turn down to medium and put the duck breast in, skin-side down. Use your hand to move the duck around the pan, preventing it from sticking as the fat renders out. Continue for 5 to 7 minutes, or until the duck skin begins to brown and duck fat pools in the pan. Remove the duck from the pan.

4. Preheat the oven to 375°F.

5. On a well-floured surface, use a rolling pin to stretch the dough square until it is about ⅛-inch thick. Place the duck breast, skin-side up, onto the dough. Spread the feta onto the skin. Fold the dough so that the sides overlap and seal at the top.

6. Prepare a sheet pan by either spraying with vegetable oil or greasing with butter. Place the dough pocket on the prepared pan, so the sealed side is on the bottom. Bake for 15 to 20 minutes, until the dough is golden brown. The duck breast should be medium-rare to medium. Serve hot.

ALBONDIGAS

Albondigas, or Spanish meatballs, are one of my favorite dishes to cook. I have a deep belief that many of the world's cuisines share the same basic principles and to me, the way the paprika and fats melt together in this dish embodies everything warm about the Mediterranean and the Middle East. Similar to "grandma's meatballs" for many Italian Americans, this version trades out an all-day simmer for warming spices, but both are packed with love.

1 LB. GROUND BEEF

½ CUP CHOPPED PARSLEY

4 GARLIC CLOVES, MINCED

2 TEASPOONS KOSHER SALT

1 TABLESPOON PAPRIKA

1 TEASPOON GROUND CLOVE

½ ONION, DICED

2 TEASPOONS CANOLA OIL

2 CUPS MARINARA SAUCE

1. Preheat oven to 400°F.

2. In a large mixing bowl, combine all of the ingredients, except the oil and marinara sauce, and mix well. Divide the mixture into 8 balls, 2 oz. each, and then roll the balls into a torpedo shape.

3. Add the oil to a large cast-iron pan over medium-high heat, heat the canola oil. When the oil begins to shimmer add the meatballs. Brown for 2 to 3 minutes on each side and then add the sauce to the pan.

4. Place the pan in the oven and bake for 10 to 15 minutes, or until the meatballs are 155°F at their center. Serve hot.

ALBONDIGAS, see page 207

YIELD: 2 SERVINGS   **TOTAL TIME:** 45 MINUTES

SCALLOP MOUSSE RAVIOLI

Caramelized onions add a layer of sweet depth to these delicate ravioli.

6 OZ. SCALLOPS

4 TABLESPOONS UNSALTED BUTTER

¼ CUP HEAVY CREAM

¾ CUP ALL-PURPOSE FLOUR, PLUS MORE AS NEEDED

1 EGG

2 TEASPOONS KOSHER SALT

½ ONION, JULIENNED

1. Remove the side muscle from the scallops by pinching the little rectangular tag that hangs off of each one and pulling.

2. Add the butter to a small frying pan over medium-high heat. After the butter has melted, allow 1 minute to heat further and then add the scallops. Turn down the heat to medium and slowly cook the scallops, approximately 5 minutes per side. The goal is to color them as little as possible, gently cooking them and leaving as pure a scallop flavor as possible.

3. Remove the scallops from the pan and place them, still hot, in a food processor (leave the butter in the pan; this will be used for the sauce). Puree the scallops and slowly drizzle in the cream to create a scallop paste. Refrigerate, uncovered.

4. In a small bowl, place ½ cup flour and create a divot in the middle. Crack the egg into the center and use a fork to break the yolk and beat the egg, folding in a bit of the flour. As the egg and flour start to become a dough mix in the rest of the flour. Knead by hand, using a little dusting of flour or a few drops of water to create a dry but stretchy dough. Cover with a towel and let rest for 5 minutes or so (or refrigerate if you are doing this step ahead of time).

5. Once the dough has rested, flour the work surface. Break the dough into 2 pieces and use a rolling pin to roll out the dough as thin as possible. I like my pasta dough to be almost see-through. Use dough cutters or a glass to cut circles of dough; I recommend 2-inch cirlces.

6. Stuff the ravioli by placing the chilled scallop mousse (about 1 teaspoon) in the middle of half of the circles and then cover each one with another circle. Use a fork to pinch the circles up against the filling, making sure no air is left in the ravioli; the air inside is what breaks them apart when they boil.

7. Bring a large pot of water to a boil. Once the water is boiling turn it down slightly, so it remains near boiling temperature but isn't rough enough to damage the ravioli. Salt the water and then place the ravioli, 5 at a time, into the water and boil for 3 to 4 minutes, or until fully softened.

8. Return the frying pan of butter back to medium-high heat. Once the butter starts to sizzle add the onions and stir frequently, allowing the onions to fully caramelize and the butter to brown.

9. Add the cooked ravioli to the onion mixture, cook for a minute or so, and then serve.

HONEY & APPLE BRAISED SHORT RIBS, see page 214

HONEY & APPLE BRAISED SHORT RIBS

These short ribs are wonderful on their own, but they are what make our Chickpea Poutine (see page 30) so popular.

1 (3 LB.) RACK OF SHORT RIBS

2 TABLESPOONS KOSHER SALT

1 TABLESPOON BLACK PEPPER

1 MEDIUM WHITE ONION, JULIENNED

2 MEDIUM APPLES, PEELED AND SLICED

¼ CUP HONEY

¼ CUP EXTRA VIRGIN OLIVE OIL

1 CUP WHITE VINEGAR

2 CUPS WATER

1. Preheat the oven to 350°F degrees.

2. Remove the connective tissue, excess fat, and silver skin from both sides of the rib rack. Coat in black pepper and salt.

3. Add the oil to a cast-iron pan, large enough to fit the rack of ribs, over medium-high heat. When the oil begins to shimmer sear both sides of the ribs until golden brown. Remove the ribs and place them into a baking pan, leaving the cast iron over heat.

4. Add the onion and apples to the pan, stirring often for 2 to 3 minutes. Turn the heat off and add the vinegar and honey. After 1 minute of stirring pour the contents of the pan over the ribs. Add the water to the pan and wrap completely in foil (plastic wrap under the foil helps but is not necessary).

5. Put the pan into the oven and cook for approximately 3 hours, or until the meat falls off the bone. Serve hot.

ROSH HASHANAH SHORT RIB

Growing up in my house the New Year always meant brisket. It was a happy time and there was a focus on apples as a traditional ingredient. All grown up I've found beauty in pairing apples with sumac. This sweet and tangy combination works especially well cutting against a rich and fatty meat like short rib. These short ribs are fall-off-the-bone tender and can be served over rice or with a starchy puree.

4-BONE RACK OF SHORT RIBS

2 TABLESPOONS KOSHER SALT

3 TABLESPOONS FRESH CRACKED BLACK PEPPER

¼ CUP EXTRA-VIRGIN OLIVE OIL

1 ONION, QUARTERED

8 GARLIC CLOVES, MINCED

2 APPLES, PEELED AND SLICED

1 TABLESPOON SUMAC

½ CUP WHITE VINEGAR

¼ CUP HONEY

1. The first, and most important, step when cooking short ribs is the trimming process. Using a sharp knife (preferably a boning knife) remove the silver skin, connective tissue, and excess fat from both sides of the ribs.

2. In a small bowl, combine the salt and pepper and mix well. Cover the entire short rib rack with the seasoning blend.

3. Preheat the oven to 400°F.

4. Set a very large pan or grill pan over high heat. After 5 minutes or so add a tablespoon of olive oil to the pan and place the short ribs, top-side down, in the pan. Let the ribs brown for 5 minutes and then brown the other side. Remove the ribs from the pan and set them in an oven-safe pan. Keep the pan over the high heat.

5. Add the onion, garlic, apples, remaining olive oil, and sumac to the same pan and sauté for a minute and then pour over the ribs. Add the vinegar to the rib and then drizzle the honey over the ribs. Cover the pan with foil, place the pan in the oven, and cook for 4 hours.

6. After 4 hours remove the pan and make sure the meat is tender. Cut the ribs between the bones and serve them each hot and on the bone.

ROSH HASHANAH SHORT RIB, see page 215

WOOD-FIRED CALAMARI, see page 220

WOOD-FIRED CALAMARI

Most folks don't have a wood-fire oven at home, but I find that this recipe can be duplicated using a very hot grill. The technique depends on very high ambient temperatures to almost air fry the squid while the sauce absorbs the grilled flavor. Like a lot of our seafood dishes, we introduce an often ignored protein into a classic Mediterranean profile here. The result is a rich and tender seafood dish perfect on its own or over pasta.

10 OZ. POINT JUDITH SQUID, RINGS AND TENTACLES

2 TABLESPOONS OLIVE OIL

1 PINT CHERRY TOMATOES

4 GARLIC CLOVES, MINCED

½ ONION, JULIENNED

1 TEASPOON UNSALTED BUTTER

1 TEASPOON KOSHER SALT

1 PINCH BLACK PEPPER

1 TABLESPOON DRY WHITE WINE

¼ CUP CHOPPED PARSLEY

1. Heat the grill as hot as possible, 500°F or above.

2. Strain the calamari.

3. Set a medium-sized frying pan on the grill and add the olive oil, tomatoes, garlic, and onion, stir to combine, and then cover the grill, checking every 3 or 4 minutes to make sure the pan has liquid in it.

4. After 10 minutes, or less if hotter (in an 800°F oven this will take approximately 6 minutes), remove the pan from the grill and add the butter, salt, pepper, wine, and parsley. Mix well and set aside.

5. Add the calamari to a separate frying pan, set it on the grill, and cover the grill.

6. After 2 minutes remove the calamari and add it to the sauce, leaving behind all of the liquid from the calamari pan. Return the calamari to the grill and cover for 2 to 3 minutes to finish. Serve hot.

DOGFISH CHRAIME

Technically a shark, dogfish is a tender white fish with a somewhat similar texture and flavor as cod or haddock. Traditionally, chraime is made as more of a fish stew, but to highlight the dogfish—a trash fish native to New England waters that if more popular could save cod from overfishing—we prepare the sauce separately and serve the fish seared.

2 TABLESPOONS EXTRA-VIRGIN OLIVE OIL, DIVIDED

½ ONION, MEDIUM DICE

2 GARLIC CLOVES, MINCED

3 TOMATOES, MEDIUM DICE

1 PINCH CUMIN

1 PINCH CAYENNE

2 TEASPOONS KOSHER SALT, DIVIDED

1 (12 OZ.) DOGFISH FILLET

1 TEASPOON BLACK PEPPER

1. Add 1 tablespoon olive oil to a medium frying pan over medium-high heat. When the oil begins to shimmer add the onion and garlic. Sauté for approximately 2 minutes and then add the tomatoes, cumin, cayenne, and 1 teaspoon salt. Stir and allow to simmer on medium-high heat until the tomatoes are broken down. In the event that the tomatoes are not juicy enough to keep the sauce building, add a small amount of water to prevent the sauce from burning.

2. Cut the fillet in half, shortening the long skinny filet, and season with the salt and pepper.

3. Add the remainder of the olive oil to a separate frying pan over high heat. When the oil begins to shimmer add the fish, bottom-side down. Allow the fish to brown, about 2 minutes, and then carefully flip it, cooking for another few minutes, until the fish reaches 145°F or until the flesh is opaque all the way through.

4. To serve, spoon the sauce into a shallow bowl, place the fillets on top of the sauce, and then spoon a small amount of sauce onto the fish.

DOGFISH CHRAIME, see page 221

MARINATED FLANK STEAK

Often considered a "butcher's cut" flank steak is a favorite cut of mine because of its willingness to easily accept marinating. I like to use a bright acid – lemon juice, lime, white vinegar – when marinating anything and this recipe builds around our Green Zhoug for an herb-heavy, bright flavor. Keep in mind that, like any meat with a pronounced grain, how you cut the flank after it's cooked is as important as how you cook it.

1 (30-40 OZ.) FLANK STEAK

1 CUP GREEN ZHOUG (SEE PAGE 101)

2 TABLESPOONS WHITE VINEGAR

1 TABLESPOON HONEY

1 TABLESPOON KOSHER SALT

1 TABLESPOON BLACK PEPPER

1. In a small bowl, combine the zhoug, vinegar, and honey and mix well.

2. Coat the steak with the marinade and place the meat in a 2 lb. sealable freezer bag. Refrigerate the meat for at least 2 hours and up to 24 hours.

3. When ready to cook the steak preheat the oven to 400°F and set a cast-iron pan over high heat

4. Sear the steak on all 4 sides for 3 minutes per side and then place the pan in the oven and cook to the desired temperature; my preference is medium for flank steak.

5. Once the steak has reached temperature, set it on a cutting board and rest for at least 5 minutes, and up to 15 minutes.

6. To serve, use a sharp knife to cut the flank steak against the grain. This usually involves two cuts: first cut the steak into sections the width of your desired steak lengths if necessary.

YEMENITE FRIED CHICKEN

For a lot of regulars and food writers, our Yemenite Fried Chicken is the signature dish at Simcha. For me, it was a dish that embodied the spirit of our team and the soul of what we were trying to do at the restaurant. It was just enough like Nashville Hot Chicken to be familiar and capture the hearts of less adventurous eaters for whom Simcha's menu could be intimidating, while also being uniquely delicious enough to rival our most outside-the-box creations. I've often remarked to the staff that the dishes that seem to resonate the most with our guests are the ones where we've done the least. I guess the age-old adage is true, sometimes less is more.

1 WHOLE CHICKEN

4 CUPS WATER

4 TABLESPOONS KOSHER SALT

¼ CUP RED ZHOUG (SEE PAGE 99)

1 QUART CANOLA OIL, FOR FRYING

2 CUPS CHICKPEA FLOUR

2 CUPS YEMENITE HOT SAUCE (SEE PAGE 111)

1. Leaving the skin on, break down the chicken, separating the legs, thighs, and breasts. The legs and thighs will be bone-in while the breast will be boneless.

2. In a large refrigerator-friendly bowl with a lid mix the water, salt, and zhoug. Place the 6 pieces of chicken into the brine, making sure to cover all of the chicken completely. For best results brine the chicken in the refrigerator with the lid on for 6 hours.

3. Remove the chicken from the refrigerator and rinse thoroughly. Clean the container and then place the chicken back in it and cover it in water; this step will ensure that the chicken remains juicy but will not be unpleasantly salty. After at least 2 hours of desalinating the chicken, and up to 24 hours, remove the chicken from the water.

4. Heat canola oil over high heat in a deep pan or medium-size pot. The desired temperature should be 350°F. When the oil is hot enough, coat the chicken one piece at a time in the chickpea flour, using a medium-sized bowl. Place the coated pieces of chicken into the hot oil, turning as necessary, for 8 to 10 minutes. Internal temperatures should be above 165°F. Place on a cooling rack to remove any excess oil.

5. Once the chicken has been fried submerge each piece one at a time in the hot sauce and serve hot.

EGGPLANT ROLLATINI, see page 230

EGGPLANT ROLLATINI

Despite the perception that Israeli cuisine is heavy on vegetarian recipes, we struggle at Simcha to create vegetarian entrees. Elevating vegetables in salad or small plate form is much simpler than in entree form, simply because there needs to be something hearty in an entree and many Middle Eastern dishes use lamb or beef to achieve that. This rollatini is Italian influenced, and breaded like my grandmother would make her schnitzel. The sumac adds an astringent aspect that I love.

1 MEDIUM EGGPLANT

2 EGGS

½ CUP ALL-PURPOSE FLOUR

1 CUP PANKO

2 CUPS CANOLA OIL, FOR FRYING

1 CUP RICOTTA CHEESE

1 TEASPOON SUMAC

1 TEASPOON SUGAR

1 TEASPOON FRESH LEMON JUICE

1 TABLESPOON KOSHER SALT

2 CUPS MARINARA SAUCE

1. Slice off the top of the eggplant and then slice it into ¼-inch-thick planks from the top of the eggplant to the bottom.

2. In a long, shallow container, beat the eggs. Pour the flour and panko onto two separate plates.

3. Add oil to a shallow frying pan over medium-high heat.

4. Coat the eggplant, first covering each plank with flour, then egg, and then panko, making sure each piece is fully coated.

5. Fry the coated eggplant for about 2 minutes per side. Remove from the oil and place on a cooling rack. Repeat until all of the eggplant is fried.

6. Preheat the oven to 400°F.

7. In a medium bowl, combine the remainder of the ingredients, except the sauce, and mix well.

8. With each eggplant slice facing vertically away from you, put a heaping tablespoon of the mixture onto the eggplant so that it spans from one side to the other the short way, and roll up the eggplant. Place the rolled eggplant into a cast-iron pan, seam-side down. Repeat for each eggplant slice, placing the rolled eggplant slices against each other to hold them in place while they cook. When they are done being rolled pour the tomato sauce over them.

9. Bake for 25 to 30 minutes, or until the filling is warmed through. Remove each piece carefully with a spatula and serve hot.

LOBSTER TAHDIG

Tahdig is a communal dish, usually made in bulk and served to the table as a whole. At its core it is a simple dish, crispy on the outside and creamy on the inside. The lobster and the Smoked Egg Aioli make this version decadent, an interesting way to eat both tahdig and lobster.

2 WHOLE LIVE LOBSTERS

1 CUP RAW RICE

2 TABLESPOONS UNSALTED BUTTER

½ WHITE ONION, FINELY DICED

¼ CUP CHOPPED PARSLEY

2 TABLESPOONS SOUR CREAM

1 TEASPOON KOSHER SALT

1 TABLESPOON SMOKED EGG AIOLI (SEE PAGE 102)

1. Bring a large pot of water to a boil. Place the two lobsters into the pot and cover. After 8 to 10 minutes remove the lobsters and place them directly into an ice bath. Once the lobsters are cool enough to handle, crack the lobster shell and remove the meat from the tail, claws, and knuckles.

2. In another large pot boil 5 cups of water. Once the water is boiling add the rice and boil for about 15 minutes, until the rice is tender enough to eat. Strain and set aside.

3. Add 1 tablespoon of butter toa medium-sized frying pan over medium heat. When the butter begins to foam, add the onions and the parsley. After 3 or 4 minutes, as the onions become translucent, add the meat from the knuckles and claws, and fold in your rice. Next mix in the sour cream and salt.

4. Add the remainder of the butter to a small saucepan over medium-high heat. When the butter begins to foam add the lobster tails to the pan and cover them with the rice mixture. Pack the pan full, pressing down. Cook for 5 to 7 minutes, or until the rice is browned on the outsides – you'll be able to smell this more than see it.

5. Remove from heat and, by placing a plate topside down on top of the saucepan and then turning both upside down, remove the tahdig onto the plate. Scrape out any pieces that stick and place them on top.

6. To serve, top with the aioli.

LOBSTER TAHDIG, see page 231

DESSERTS

Everybody loves a sweet ending to a delicious meal. If you can master desserts, you can always leave your guests with a final impression that elevates the memory of any meal. At Simcha, we try to craft desserts that are unusual without being overly complicated or intricate. Play with flavors, but be delicate, and your desserts will be perfect.

KENTUCKY BOURBON PECAN PIE BAKLAVA

Baklava was the first dessert I ever sold professionally. It's easy to make—time-consuming, but easy—and lends itself to all kinds of creativity. I created this version for a food truck festival where we were challenged to incorporate Maker's Mark into dishes. My Grandma Alice was a big-time pecan pie fan, and this baklava feels to me like a little bit of both sides of my family.

2 CUPS BROWN SUGAR, DIVIDED

1 TEASPOON VANILLA EXTRACT

1 TEASPOON CINNAMON

1 PINCH CLOVES

16 OZ. PECANS

1 CUP UNSALTED BUTTER, MELTED AND DIVIDED

½ LB. PHYLLO DOUGH, THAWED

1 CUP WATER

3 OZ. MAKER'S MARK BOURBON

1. In a food processor, combine 1 cup brown sugar, vanilla, cinnamon, cloves, pecans, and ½ cup melted butter to form a somewhat clumpy filling.

2. Using half a box of phyllo dough, cut the sheets in half, from 18"x13" to 9"x13". Use a pastry brush to spread one thin layer of butter across a 9"x13" sheet pan. Lay down the first sheet of phyllo. Repeat this step, lightly buttering each sheet before laying the next sheet on top. After 9 sheets have been laid down it is time to spread the filling.

3. Evenly distribute the filling, covering the entire rectangle. Make sure this layer is very even.

4. Place a sheet of phyllo dough on top of the filling without butter underneath. This layer will need to be a little more saturated with butter on top than the others. Now continue to layer the rest of the sheets.

5. Preheat the oven to 350°F. Using a very sharp knife cut the baklava. I cut triangles, so first I cut the pan in half, then each section in half, and so on until I have the size baklava I want. I cut all the squares diagonally at the end to give me triangles. It is very important that this is done before baking.

6. Bake for 40 to 45 minutes, or until golden brown.

7. While the baklava is in the oven, add the water, bourbon, and the remainder of the brown sugar to a small saucepan and bring to a boil. Reduce temperature to medium-high heat and allow to reduce by ⅓. This syrup will be poured over the baklava once it is done baking.

8. Allow the baklava to cool and serve at room temperature.

BLUEBERRY & GINGER MALABI, opposite
SPICY CHOCOLATE HALVAH, see page 240

BLUEBERRY & GINGER MALABI

Malabi is a traditional thickened milk dessert eaten throughout the Middle East. At Simcha, we thicken it quite a bit and serve it like a panna cotta. This flavor is one of my favorites, but you can swap in any flavor combo you'd like.

2 CUPS LIGHT CREAM

1 TABLESPOON WHITE SUGAR

1 TEASPOON GRATED GINGER

½ CUP BLUEBERRIES

¼ CUP COLD WATER

2 TABLESPOONS CORNSTARCH

1. Add the cream, sugar, ginger, and blueberries to a small saucepan over medium heat. When the mixture begins to bubble at the sides turn it down to low and simmer for 30 minutes.

2. Using an immersion blender or a food processor (careful, the hot liquid will rise and spill over) blend the mixture and then strain. Once the liquid has been a strained return it to the pot and set it over medium-high heat.

3. In a small bowl, combine the water and cornstarch and slowly stir the slurry into the cream mixture. As the cream thickens lower the heat to medium and, after 5 minutes, or when the cream turns to a pudding consistency, remove from heat.

4. Separate into 4 even portions (I use 4 oz. mason jars) and refrigerate for 4 hours. Serve cold.

SPICY CHOCOLATE HALVAH

As a kid, halvah was the coolest thing about having an Israeli dad. My cousins would bring it with them when they visited (and Bamba, and Beasly) and we'd gobble it all up. Halvah is somewhat simple to make, the temperature of the sugar syrup will impact the texture drastically though. Lower temperature and it will be like oily fudge, higher temperatures will lead to hard, flaky halvah. I aim for a solid but soft candy.

1 CUP TAHINI

1 CUP SUGAR

1 CUP WATER

3 OZ. DARK CHOCOLATE

1 TEASPOON CAYENNE

1. Add the tahini to a small saucepan over medium heat and warm.

2. Add the sugar and water to a separate small saucepan over high heat and bring to a boil. and boil the sugar and water on high. Using a candy thermometer, bring the sugar water to 265°F. Before you get there though, the tahini will have to be ready.

3. As you wait for the sugar water to reach temperature, add the chocolate and cayenne to the tahini, melting the chocolate.

4. Once the sugar water reaches 265°F, immediately remove it from the heat and stir it into the tahini. Incorporate the sugar syrup quickly and don't over mix, that will cause cracking.

5. Pour the mixture into a container the shape of which you want the halvah. I use silicone molds, small loaf pans, or Tupperware containers. The halvah should set relatively quickly (30 minutes or less) and can be kept in the refrigerator for up to 2 weeks. Serve at room temperature.

YIELD: 2 SERVINGS   **TOTAL TIME**: 1 HOUR, PLUS 5 DAYS FOR FERMENTATION

FERMENTED BANANA FRITTERS

Fermenting bananas is something I like to do for a variety of baked goods, but these fritters are the easiest and we always have them on the menu at Simcha. Once you know what to watch out for, it's a very easy and straightforward process, and the fritters themselves benefit from the fermentation, which makes them airy and crispy.

2 BANANAS

1 TEASPOON DRY ACTIVE YEAST

2 CUPS WATER

½ CUP ALL-PURPOSE FLOUR

1 TEASPOON BAKING POWDER

2 CUPS CANOLA OIL, FOR FRYING

2 TABLESPOONS PEANUT BUTTER

2 TABLESPOONS SUGAR

1 TABLESPOON CINNAMON

1. Peel the bananas, slice them into ½-inch pieces, and place them in a mason jar. Add the yeast and then cover the bananas completely with the water. Cover the jar and set it in a cupboard, keeping it at roughly 70°F, for 4 to 5 days. The bananas should smell a little like alcohol but not funky, and any bananas at the top that brown should be thrown away. Generally, I describe fermented bananas as tasting the most like a banana that you've ever had.

2. Once the bananas have fermented, they can be removed from the water and mushed up in a medium-sized bowl. Add the flour and baking powder and stir to incorporate thoroughly.

3. Add the oil to a medium saucepan over high heat. Once the oil is hot, scoop tablespoon-sized balls of the batter into the oil (an ice cream scoop works great). Allow the fritters to puff and brown on one side, then flip them over and allow to brown on the other side, approximately 1½ to 2 minutes per side.

4. Melt the peanut butter in the microwave or in small frying pan over medium heat.

5. In a small bowl combine the sugar and cinnamon. When the fritters come out of the oil hot, toss them in the bowl, coating them in the mixture.

6. To serve, spread the melted peanut butter on a small plate and pile the fritters onto the plate.

BLACK LIME & STRAWBERRY CROSTATA, see page 244

BLACK LIME & STRAWBERRY CROSTATA

Acid. It's one of my favorite, if not my favorite, thing to cook with. Black limes have the most interesting acidity—they're almost like Sour Patch Kids. In this recipe, we combine that tartness with fresh strawberries to make the jam that fills a pie crust. It's a pretty little Mediterranean dessert that's relatively easy to make and everyone will enjoy.

1¾ CUPS ALL-PURPOSE FLOUR

1 CUP SUGAR, DIVIDED

1 TEASPOON BAKING POWDER

2 EGGS, AT ROOM TEMPERATURE

10 TABLESPOONS UNSALTED BUTTER, AT ROOM TEMPERATURE

2 BLACK LIMES

1 CUP WATER

1 CUP SLICED FRESH STRAWBERRIES

1. In a large bowl combine the flour, ½ cup sugar, and the baking powder. Mix well. Make a well in the center of the bowl and add 1 egg and the yolk of the second egg (reserving the egg white for the egg wash). Whisk them and incorporate them into the flour. Cut the butter into small pieces and incorporate them as well.

2. Remove the dough from the bowl and knead it into a soft ball. Wrap with plastic wrap and refrigerate for at least 30 minutes.

3. Open the black limes and pull the sticky pith from inside it. In a small saucepan, add the remainder of the sugar, 1 cup water, the strawberries, and the pith from the black limes to a saucepan over high heat and bring to a boil. Continue to boil until the mixture reduces and comes to 220°F. Remove from the heat and let cool.

4. When you're ready to work with the dough, preheat the oven to 350°F. Take the dough from the refrigerator and place it on a well-floured surface. With a rolling pin, roll the dough to ⅛". Place dough into an 8" pie pan, trimming the edges. Fill with the jam. Cut strips from the remaining dough and lay them in a lattice over the top. Brush the top of the pie crust with the reserved egg white. Bake for 30 minutes or until golden brown.

5. Cool on a cooling rack and serve at room temperature.

GOAT CHEESE & HONEY PANNA COTTA

This simple dessert shines because of the fruit garnish. Use the freshest, in-season fruit available.

2 TABLESPOONS WATER

1 ENVELOPE UNFLAVORED GELATIN

20 OZ. HEAVY CREAM

4 OZ. CREAMY GOAT CHEESE

½ CUP HONEY

1. Add the water to a small saucepan over medium heat and sprinkle the gelatin over the water and thoroughly mix. Very quickly it will become a paste; remove from heat as soon as it does. Set aside.

2. Add the cream to another small saucepan over medium heat and warm the cream. Stir in the goat cheese, fully dissolving it into the cream, and then do the same with the honey.

3. Over low heat, slowly add the cream mixture to the dissolved gelatin, making sure to fully incorporate the gelatin. Once all of the cream mixture has been added, turn up the heat to medium and cook for 10 minutes or so, stirring often to prevent any burning.

4. Remove from heat and pour into 4 oz. mason jars (though any container will do) and transfer to the refrigerator. Allow 4 to 5 hours to set.

5. Serve cold, garnished with fresh fruit and honey.

CAMPFIRE PEACHES & CREAM

Here is another example of how grilling food can be more about flavoring it than cooking it. At the height of a New England summer, this dessert is a showstopper.

1 PINT HEAVY WHIPPING CREAM

2 TABLESPOONS HONEY

1 PINCH CLOVES

4 PEACHES, HALVED

1 HAZELNUT

1. Heat the grill to high.

2. Combine the cream, honey, and clove in a medium-sized bowl and whisk vigorously, until stiff peaks form. Using an electric mixer will make this process much easier.

3. Grill the peaches, turning them often and making sure they brown on all sides but do not burn.

4. Once the peaches are done, place two halves each into separate bowls and top with the whipped cream. Using a microplane or a small cheese grater, shave a hazelnut over each bowl. Serve warm.

METRIC CONVERSION CHART

U.S. Measurement	Approximate Metric Liquid Measurement	Approximate Metric Dry Measurement
1 teaspoon	5 ml	–
1 tablespoon or ½ ounce	15 ml	14 g
1 ounce or ⅛ cup	30 ml	29 g
¼ cup or 2 ounces	60 ml	57 g
⅓ cup	80 ml	–
½ cup or 4 ounces	120 ml	113 g
⅔ cup	160 ml	–
¾ cup or 6 ounces	180 ml	–
1 cup or 8 ounces or ½ pint	240 ml	227 g
1½ cups or 12 ounces	350 ml	–
2 cups or 1 pint or 16 ounces	475 ml	454 g
3 cups or 1½ pints	700 ml	–
4 cups or 2 pints or 1 quart	950 ml	–

ABOUT THE AUTHOR

ISRAELI-AMERICAN CHEF AVI SHEMTOV opened The Chubby Chickpea as a quick-serve Israeli street-food concept in 2010 in the suburbs of Boston, Massachusetts. Credited with being part of the movement to popularize Israeli cuisine globally, Shemtov launched The Chubby Chickpea Food Truck less than two years later to critical acclaim. The Chubby Chickpea continues to operate multiple food trucks and catering outlets in the Boston area.

In 2017, Shemtov formed The Shemtov Group, the umbrella under which, in addition to The Chubby Chickpea, he would open TAPPED Beer Truck (2017) Simcha (2019), Arabe Food Truck (2020), and a La Esh (2020).

Shemtov serves as Executive Chef of Simcha, located in his hometown of Sharon. Focused on New England-influenced modern Israeli menu, Simcha was named one of Boston's 15 Best New Restaurants by both *Boston Magazine* and *The Boston Globe*.

Shemtov has appeared on multiple media outlets, most notably *Simply Ming* with Chef Ming Tsai on PBS and *Henry in the Hub* on WGBH radio. In 2020, Shemtov and his team were invited to cook at the famed James Beard House in New York City. He co-hosts the podcast Heat In The Kitchen and wrote *The Single Guy Cookbook*.

In addition to his restaurant and business ventures, Shemtov currently sits on the board of Red, White and Blue Coats in his hometown, runs a school lunch program to combat food insecurity, and mentors aspiring entrepreneurs.

Shemtov lives in Sharon with his wife, Adrien, and their two children, Adley and Adina.

ABOUT CIDER MILL PRESS BOOK PUBLISHERS

Good ideas ripen with time. From seed to harvest, Cider Mill Press brings fine reading, information, and entertainment together between the covers of its creatively crafted books. Our Cider Mill bears fruit twice a year, publishing a new crop of titles each spring and fall.

"Where Good Books Are Ready for Press"

Visit us online at
cidermillpress.com

or write to us at
PO Box 454
12 Spring St.
Kennebunkport, Maine 04046